1A

1B

1C

1D

3

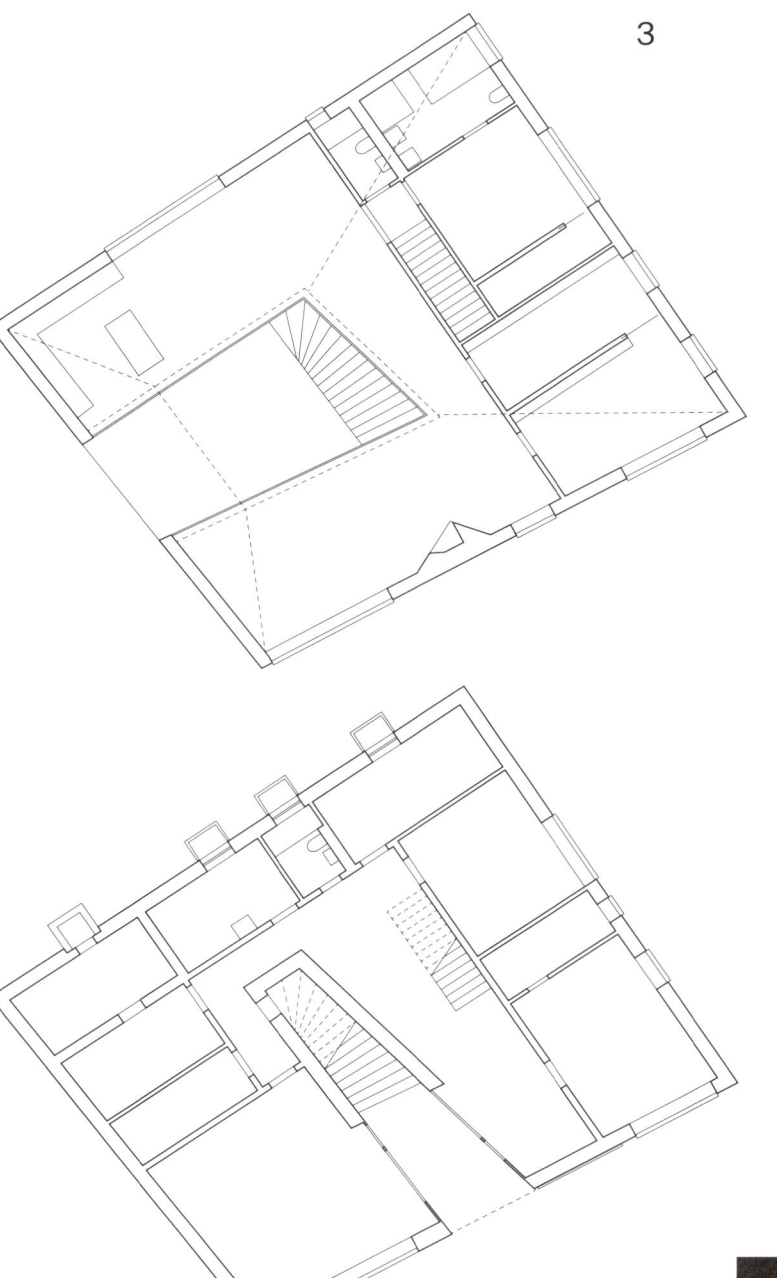

5m

1E

1F

1G

1H

1I

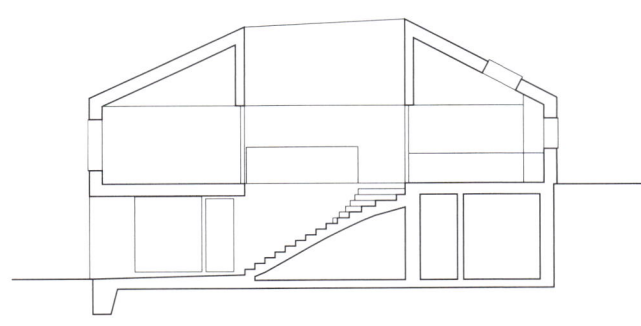 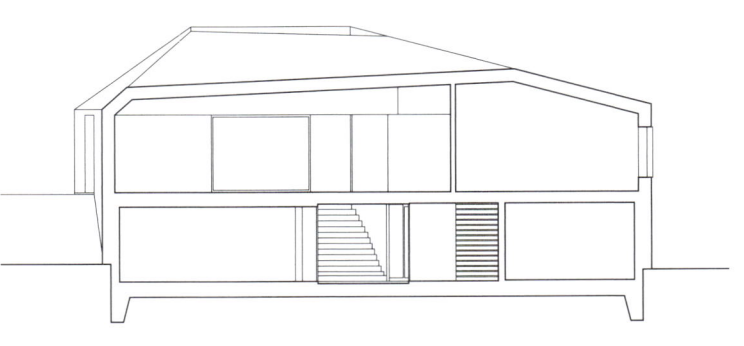

5m

1J

Wohnhaus für Künstler
Lupsingen, 2003–2005

House for Artists
Lupsingen, 2003–2005

In unmittelbarer Nähe zum Waldrand gelegen, erscheint das Wohnhaus vertraut und irritierend anders zugleich: Das Walmdach und die erdverbundene Volumetrie verorten das Gebäude im ländlichen Kontext. Das Dach ist jedoch asymmetrisch ausgebildet, es gibt weder Vordächer noch Regenrinnen, und die Schieferplatten überziehen Dach und Fassade gleichermassen. Konsequenterweise läuft das Regenwasser einfach über die Fassaden ab. Derselben Logik folgt die Verwendung von Dachflächenfenstern, die einzeln oder zu mehreren nebeneinander angeordnet sind.

Der Innenhof als räumliches Zentrum führt das Thema der Verfremdung fort: Es ist kein klassischer Patio, sondern ein typologisch hybrider Aussenraum, der vom Eingangsbereich im Sockelgeschoss über die «Sommertreppe» erschlossen wird und gegen Südwesten eine torgrosse Öffnung aufweist. Damit setzt er den tiefen Gebäudekörper von innen her unter Spannung, wozu auch die Verwendung polygonaler Formen im Grundriss wie im Schnitt beiträgt, die hier erstmals erprobt wird. Gleichwohl bleibt der in sich ruhende Charakter des Wohnhauses erhalten. Der leichte Verzug im Grundriss gibt dem Innenhof Halt, und die spezifische Geometrie des Walmdaches, der gemäss Bauordnung neben Satteldächern einzig erlaubten Dachform, wirkt zentrierend. Obwohl der Hof im Innern allgegenwärtig ist, behalten die angrenzenden Räume eine wohltuende Eigenständigkeit bei, denn die Wände sind nur bis auf die Höhe der umlaufenden Traufe in Glas aufgelöst und nicht bis unter das schräge Dach. Eine bewusste Ambivalenz zeigt sich auch in der Konstruktionsweise: Auf dem betonierten Sockelgeschoss steht ein Holzrahmenbau. Die kleinformatigen Schieferplatten wirken wie ein Mantel, der das Gebäude gegen aussen vereinheitlicht und das überraschende Innere den Blicken entzieht.

Located directly at the edge of the forest, the house appears both familiar and unsettlingly alien: the hip roof and grounded volumetry situate the building in the rural context. The roof, however, is asymmetrically articulated, there are neither canopies nor rain gutters, and the slate tiles cover both roof and façade. As a consequence rainwater simply runs off down the façade. Following the same logic, skylight windows are inserted separately, or several are organized next to each other.

As core spatial element, the inner courtyard continues the theme of alienation: rather than being a traditional patio, it is a typologically hybrid outdoor space, which is accessible from the entrance area on the plinth level via "summer stairs" and features a gate-size opening to the southwest. This configuration puts the deep volume under tension from the inside, whereby also contributing to this effect is the use of polygonal forms in the ground plan as well as section, an application which is tried out here by the architect for the first time. At the same time the character of the house remains reposed. The slight warpage in the ground plan supports the courtyard and having a centering effect is the specific geometry of the hip roof, which besides a gabled roof was the only form permitted by the building regulations. Although the courtyard is omnipresent in the interior, the adjoining rooms retain a soothing autonomy as the walls are only dissolved into glass up to the height of the encasing eaves, not all the way to the underside of the slanted roof. A conscious ambivalence is also evident in the construction method: a wood frame structure stands on the concrete plinth. The small-format slate tiles function like a coat, lending the building a unified appearance towards the outside and withdrawing the surprising interior from view.

Mitarbeit: Christoph Rothenhöfer
Tragwerksplanung: K. Bitterli + Partner Ingenieure AG, Gelterkinden
Holzbau: Pirmin Jung, Ingenieure für Holzbau, Rain
Fotos: Roger Frei (A–F, K–O), Ruedi Walti (G–J)

Staff: Christoph Rothenhöfer
Structural Engineering: K. Bitterli + Partner Ingenieure AG, Gelterkinden
Wood Construction: Pirmin Jung, Ingenieure für Holzbau, Rain
Photos: Roger Frei (A–F, K–O), Ruedi Walti (G–J)

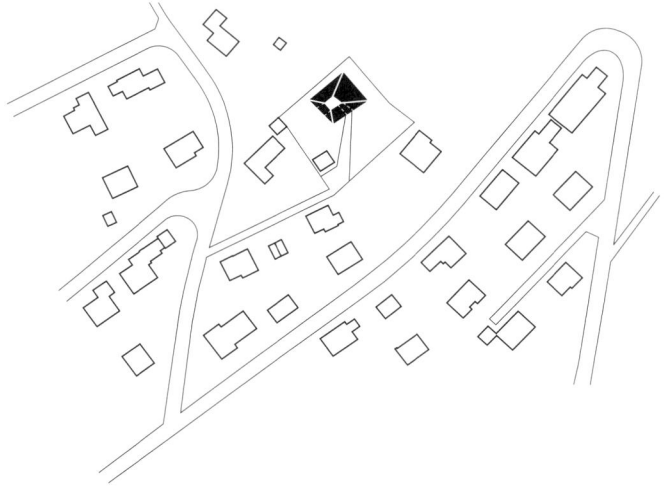

1K

1L

1M

2A

2B

2 C

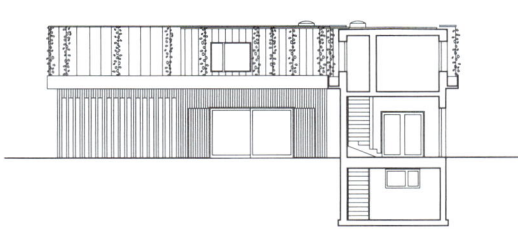 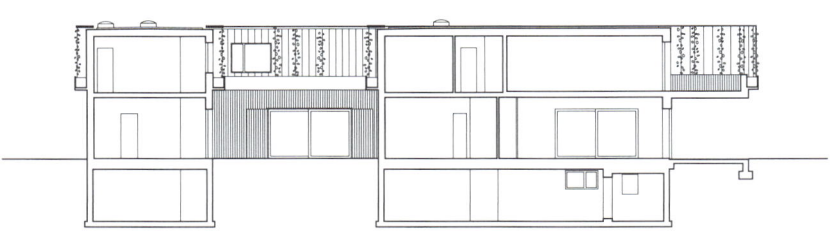

|—— 5 m

2 D

Doppelwohnhaus Bäumlihof
Riehen, 1999–2001

Bäumlihof Duplex
Riehen, 1999–2001

Das herrschaftliche Bäumlihofareal liegt in der weiten Ebene zwischen Basel und Riehen und ist über eine prächtige Kastanienallee erschlossen. Das Ensemble besteht aus dem Herrenhaus von 1686, einer historisch bedeutenden Gartenanlage aus dem 19. Jahrhundert und Ökonomiegebäuden, die Hans Bernoulli zugeschrieben werden. Hier, im ehemaligen Gemüsegarten, der als mit zahlreichen Bäumen durchsetzte Wiese interpretiert ist, befindet sich auf mäanderndem Grundriss das Doppelwohnhaus, dessen Stirnseiten im Erd- und Obergeschoss in grosszügige Terrassen aufgelöst sind. Dadurch und über die Materialisierung verbinden sich Natur und Bauwerk zu einer Einheit. Während das Erdgeschoss des Holzrahmenbaus mit einer stehenden Lärchenholzschalung verkleidet ist, knüpft die Kupferverkleidung des Obergeschosses stimmungsmässig an die Ziegeldächer des nahen Ökonomiegebäudes an. Zwischen Garten- und Obergeschoss sind mit Kupfer verkleidete und mit Erde gefüllte Tröge angeordnet, die rund um das Gebäude laufen. An Drähten wachsen Pflanzen empor, die mit dem Regenwasser versorgt werden, das auf dem Dach anfällt und über die Kupferfassade in die Rinnenkörper geleitet wird. Dieses poetische Moment wird in dem einen Hausteil durch ein Thema ergänzt, das der amerikanische Künstler Donald Judd in seinem Atelier-Wohnhaus an der Spring Street in New York und 1993 in Eichholteren am Vierwaldstättersee angewendet hat: Böden und Decken sind mit Holz belegt, die Wände dagegen hell gestrichen, sodass die Räume in Flächen aufgelöst werden und eine starke Beziehung zwischen den beiden horizontalen Ebenen entsteht. Auf diese Weise wird auch der Aussenraum der ebenerdigen Terrasse optisch zusammengehalten, ohne dass dazu Wände nötig sind.

Mitarbeit: Katrin Urwyler
Holzbau: Louis Risi AG, Allschwil
Fotos: Ruedi Walti

The manorial Bäumlihof estate lies in the wide lowlands between Basel and Riehen, and its entrance is marked by a magnificent chestnut tree alley. The ensemble consists of the manor house of 1686, 19th-century gardens of historic significance and agricultural buildings attributed to Hans Bernoulli. Here in the former kitchen garden — which has been reinterpreted as a meadow with interspersed trees — is situated on a meandering ground plan the duplex, whose front faces dissolve into spacious terraces on the ground and upper levels. Through this articulation and the materialization nature and architecture fuse into a unity. While the ground floor of the timber frame construction is clad with standing or vertical larch boards, the copper cladding of the upper level echoes the tiled roofs of the nearby agricultural building. Positioned between the ground-floor garden level and upper story, copper-clad, earth-filled troughs surround the entire building. Supplied with rainwater that runs off the roof and is directed over the copper façade into gutters, plants grow climbing up on wires. This poetic moment is complemented by incorporating in one part of the house a theme which the American artist Donald Judd used in his studio-house on Spring Street in New York as well as in Eichholteren at Lake Lucerne in 1993: floors and ceiling are finished in wood with the walls painted contrastingly in light colors so that the spaces dissolve into surfaces and strong connection between the two horizontal planes emerges. In the same way the outdoor space of the ground level terrace is held together optically without needing walls.

Staff: Katrin Urwyler
Wood Construction: Louis Risi AG, Allschwil
Photos: Ruedi Walti

2 E

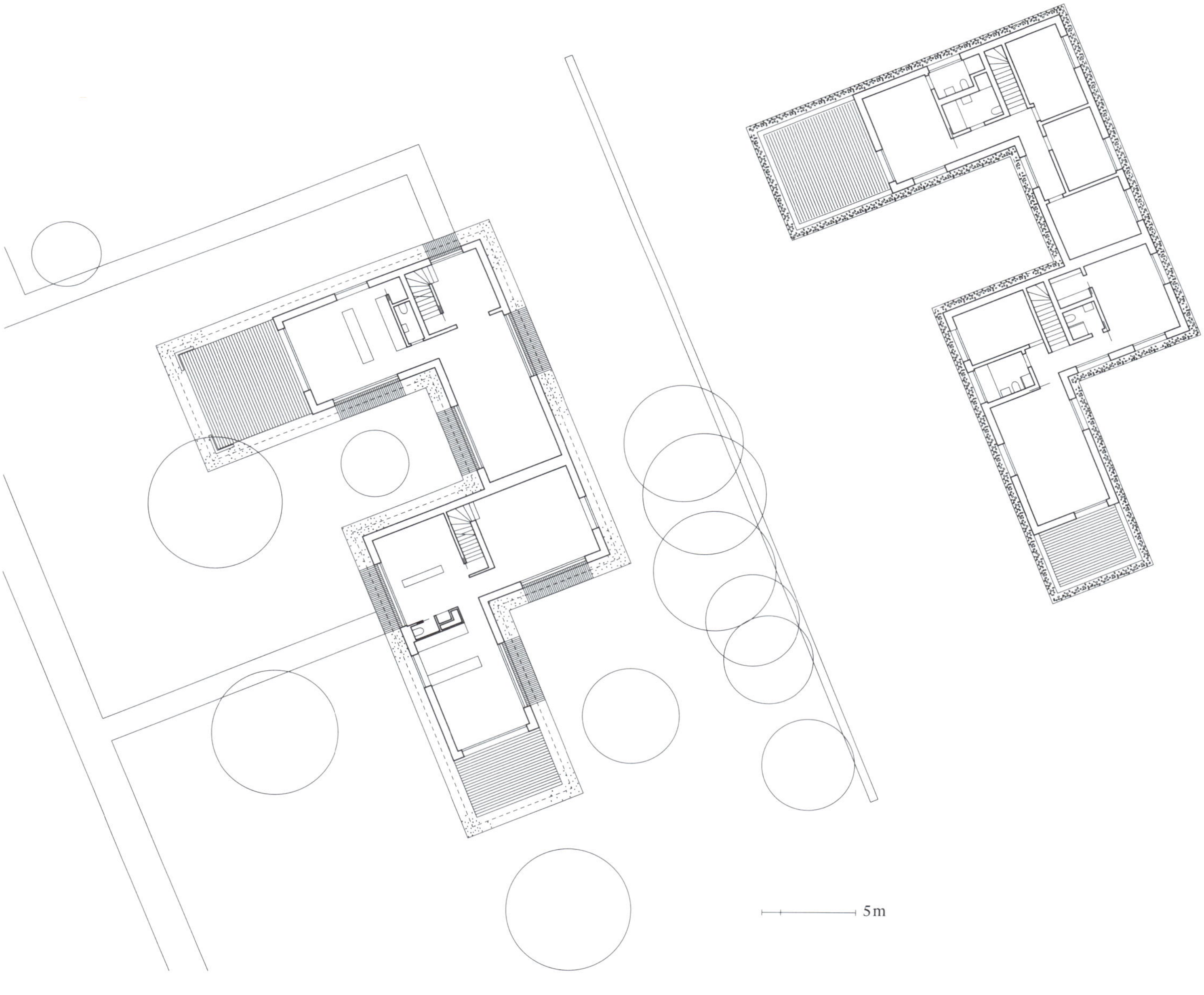

5 m

2F

2G

14

2H

2I

2J

3B

3C

3D

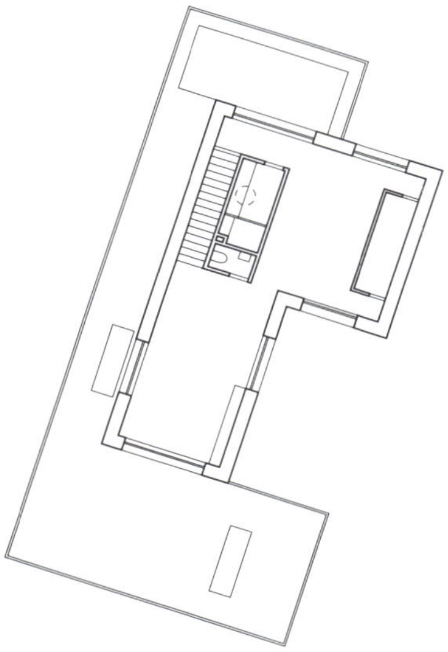

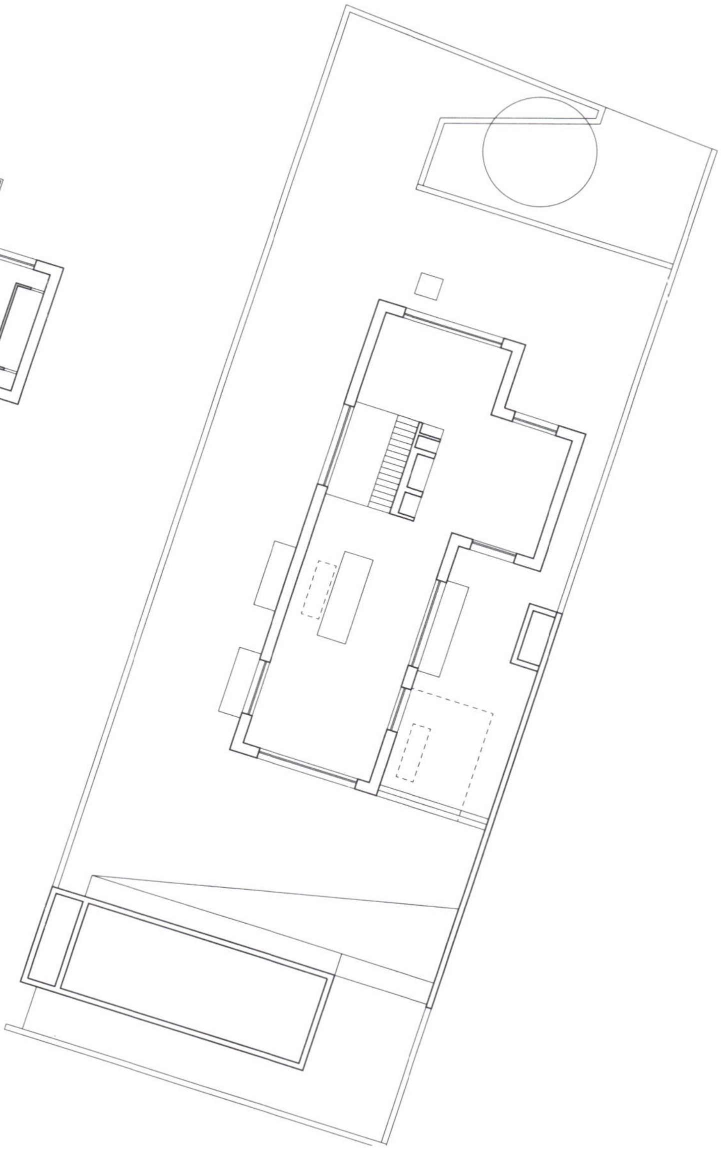

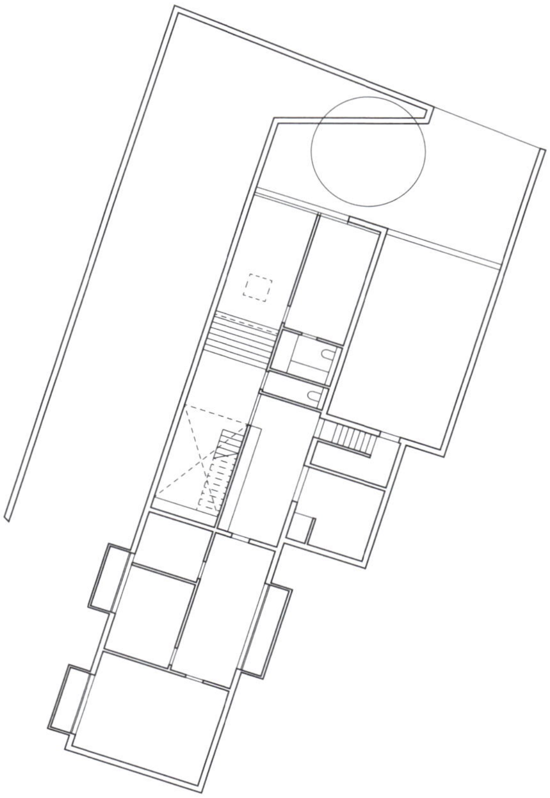

5m

Wohnhaus beim Wenkenpark
Riehen, 2002–2004

House at Wenkenpark
Riehen, 2002–2004

Die schmale Parzelle beim Wenkenpark am Dorfrand von Riehen galt als schwierig zu bebauen. Dank geschickter Staffelung des Volumens und präzise gesetzten Öffnungen spürt man davon nichts mehr, im Gegenteil: Die topografische Situation mit der Aussichtsseite im Norden und dem gegen Süden ansteigenden Hang verleiht der offenen, durch keine Türen unterbrochenen Raumfolge zusätzliche Dynamik. Vom Eingangsgeschoss, das nur stirnseitig aus dem Terrain geschnitten ist, führt eine einläufige Treppe ins Parterre und von dort ins Schlafgeschoss. Die primäre Bewegungsrichtung im Haus erfolgt längs, sodass die gegensätzlichen Lichtstimmungen im Norden und Süden stets präsent sind. Mittels Zonierung der Flächen, insbesondere durch das Treppenhaus, das ein seitliches, erkerartiges «Ausweichen» des Volumens provoziert, und die mit Fenstern durchbrochenen Längsseiten, werden aber auch Sichtbezüge in Querrichtung und über die Diagonalen hergestellt. Der erlebte Raum befreit sich damit auf überraschende Weise von der orthogonalen Struktur.

Die Fenster sind so platziert, dass die dicht stehenden benachbarten Gebäude weitgehend ausgeblendet werden. Das Wohnhaus ist mit Wittmunder Klinker gebaut, der immer in Längsrichtung verlegt ist. Damit entstehen an den Längs- und Stirnfassaden unterschiedliche Mauerwerksverbände, die die Parzellenform betonen. Die leicht schwingenden und knarrenden Holzböden aus sieben Meter langen Riemen sowie alle Schreinerarbeiten inklusive Fenster sind in Eiche gefertigt. Wie ein hölzernes Band geht das Treppengeländer in die Brüstung über und mutiert anschliessend zum Einbaumöbel. In dieser Kontinuität spiegelt sich auf der Detailebene das in aller Konsequenz umgesetzte Prinzip des Einraumhauses wieder.

The narrow plot at Wenkenpark at the outskirts of Riehen was considered difficult to build on. On account of the skillfully arranged volumes and precisely placed openings, this former presumption is no longer to be sensed, on the contrary: the topographical situation with viewing side to the north and ascending slope to the south lend further dynamic to the open spatial sequence, which no door interrupts. From the entrance level, which has only been cut out of the terrain at the front, a single flight of stairs leads to the parterre and from there to the bedroom level. The main direction of movement in the house proceeds lengthwise so that the oppositional interplay of the different moods of north-south lighting is always present. Through zoning of the surface planes — especially by means of the staircase that provokes a lateral, bay-like "shirking" of the volume and longitudinal sides that have been punctuated with windows — lateral and diagonal visual connections have also been created. The resulting effect is that the experienced space disengages itself from the orthogonal structure in a surprising way.

The windows have been so positioned that the densely neighboring buildings are largely hidden from view. The house is executed in clinker manufactured by Wittmunder Klinker, which is always clad lengthways. The resulting different brickwork courses at the longitudinal and front façades accentuate the form of the plot. The slightly swaying and creaking wood floors out of seven-meter-long planks as well as all the other carpentry work — including windows — are executed in oak. Like a wooden ribbon the stair banister transforms into a balustrade and eventually mutates into built-in furniture. This continuity — manifested in the details — reflects the absolutely consequential application of the principle of the one room house.

Mitarbeit: Katrin Urwyler
Tragwerksplanung: ZPF Ingenieure AG, Basel
Fotos: Ruedi Walti (A–C), Adriano A. Biondo (D–H)

Staff: Katrin Urwyler
Structural Engineering: ZPF Ingenieure AG, Basel
Photos: Ruedi Walti (A–C), Adriano A. Biondo (D–H)

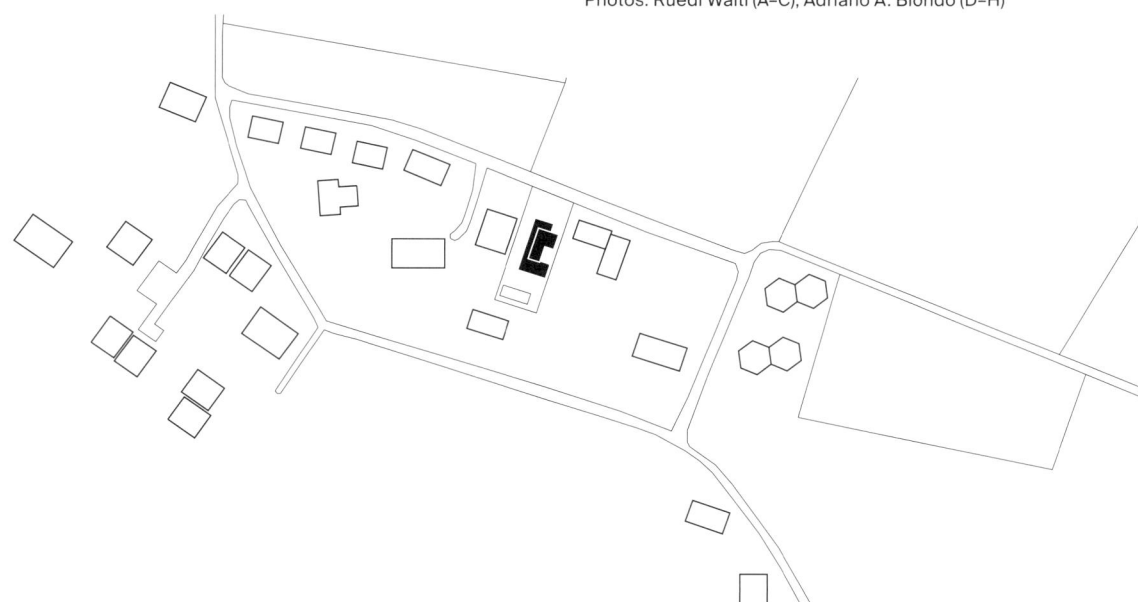

3E

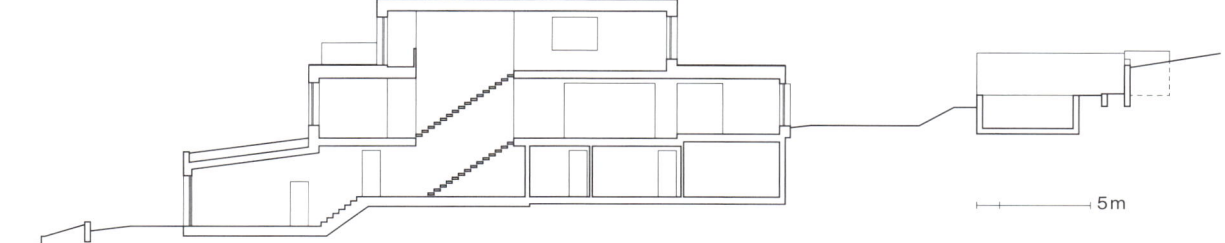

5m

3F

3G

4 A

4 B

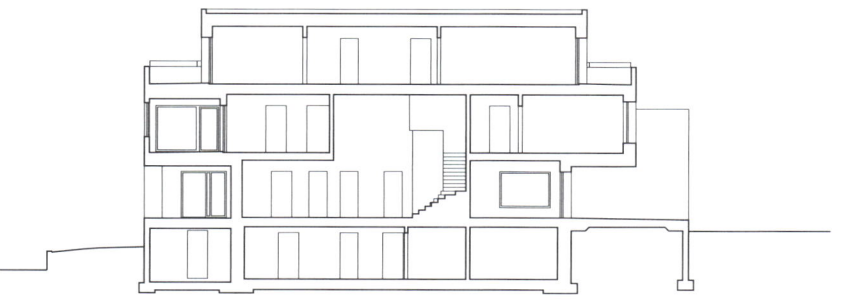

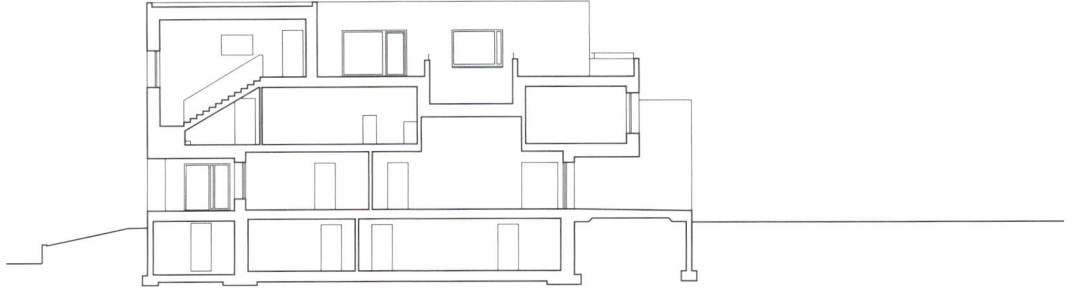

4 E

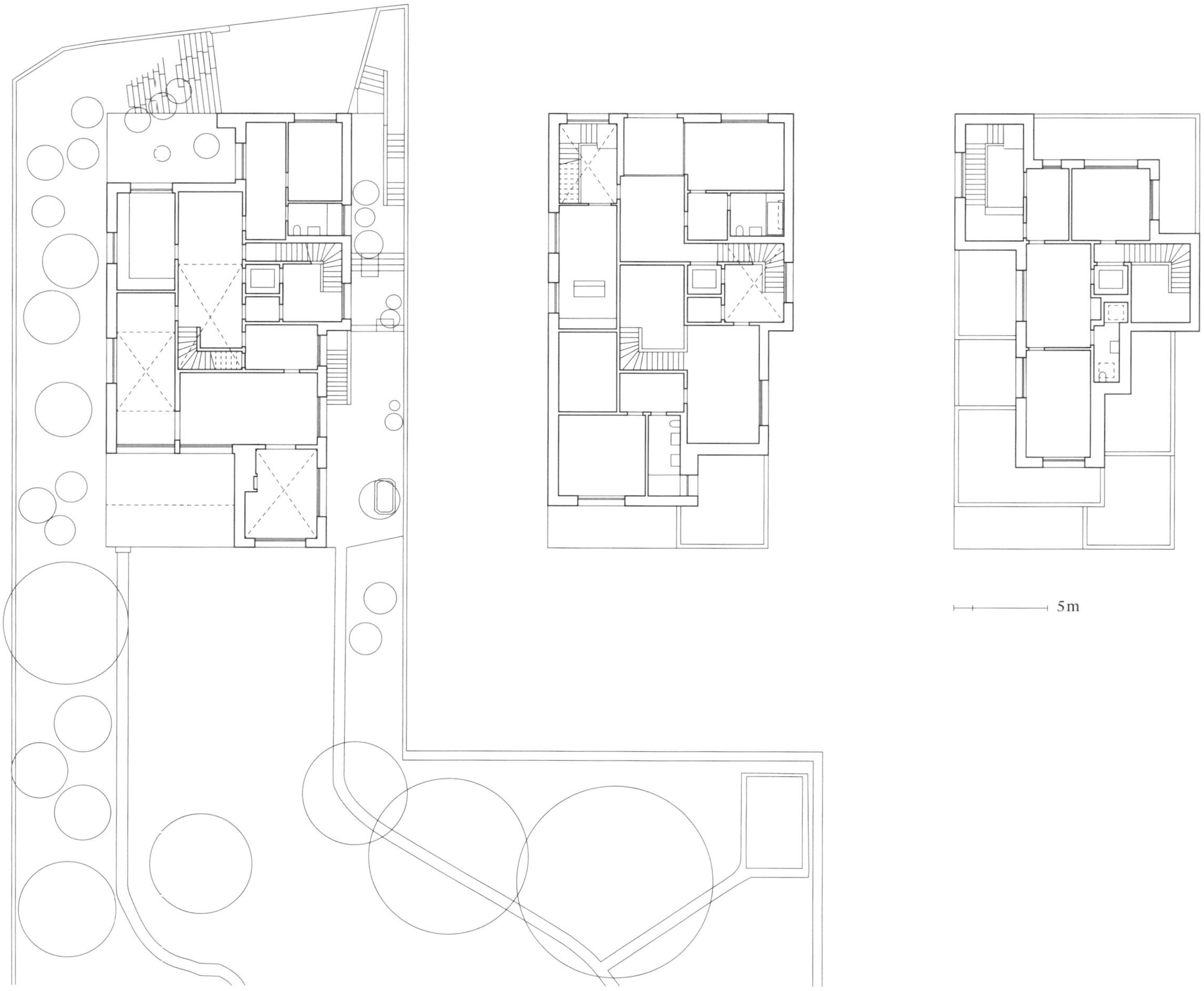

Generationenhaus
Binningen, 2010–2013

Generational House
Binningen, 2010–2013

Die stattliche Villa mit klar geschnittener, vielgestaltiger Kubatur in Weissbeton interpretiert die Körnung des Quartiers mit den strassenbegleitenden Häusern in hellen Tönen auf selbstverständliche Weise. Der Neubau ist an die nördliche Kante des parkähnlichen Grundstücks geschoben. Damit profitiert er vom freien Blick auf Basel und vom prächtigen Baumbestand. Unterschiedlich grosse Öffnungen verweisen in ihrer scheinbar freien Setzung auf das raumplanartige Innenleben, das ansonsten gegen aussen verborgen bleibt.

Umso überraschender entwickeln sich im Innern die zwei völlig unterschiedlichen Wohnungen über alle Geschosse und in jede Himmelsrichtung. Die Verschachtelung im Grundriss wie im Schnitt basiert auf einer Längsteilung der Geschossflächen in drei Schichten. Die gekammerte Raumstruktur begreift zwar jedes Zimmer als Einheit, mittels Durchblicken und räumlichen Verbindungen schafft sie gleichwohl zusammenhängende Sequenzen. Der repräsentative Bereich der elterlichen Wohnung (F–I, M–P) ist auf das Erdgeschoss mit der grosszügigen Abfolge von Ess-, Wohn- und Cheminéezimmer und der Bibliothek im Obergeschoss beschränkt, die mit der teilweise doppelgeschossigen Halle im Zentrum des Hauses verbunden ist. Deutlich davon abgetrennt sind die übrigen Räume, insbesondere das Arbeitszimmer im Attikageschoss mit separater Erschliessung. Für die erwachsenen Kinder ist die zweite Wohnung (E, J–L) ebenfalls in private und gemeinschaftliche Bereiche unterteilt, wobei hier die Zuordnungen weniger fix sind.

Die sorgfältige Detaillierung steht im Dienst gediegener Wohnlichkeit und Langlebigkeit auf höchstem handwerklichem Niveau. Die Sichtschale des Tragwerks besteht aus sehr hellem Weissbeton. Fenster und Türen sind in Baubronze ausgeführt, aufgrund der Firmenschliessung des Herstellers die letzten ihrer Art. Für die Böden wurden Eichenparkett und istrischer Kalkstein verwendet, der in grossformatigen Platten in Sand verlegt wurde. Ausgesuchte Wände sind farbig oder weiss glänzend gestrichen, sodass überraschende Tiefenwirkungen oder Lichtreflexe entstehen. Dadurch und über die spannungsreiche Platzierung der Fenster und Proportionierung der Zimmer entstehen Wohnungen von höchst individuellem Zuschnitt, die das Haus fest mit der Lebensweise ihrer Bewohner verbinden.

In a matter-of-fact way the clear-cut, multifaceted cubature of the stately villa in white concrete interprets the texture of the neighborhood with its light-toned houses lining the streets. The new building is shoved to the northernmost edge of the park-like plot and consequently profits from an unobstructed view over Basel as well as a magnificent stand of trees. The seemingly free setting of differently sized openings hints at the *Raumplan*-like inner life, which otherwise remains hidden to the outside.

Therefore the two completely different apartments that develop inside on all floors and in every direction are all the more surprising. The interweaving in ground plan as well as in section is based on a longitudinal division of the levels' surface area into three layers. While the chambered spatial structure conceives each room as a unit, it simultaneously creates cohesive sequences by means of "through-views" and spatial connections. The representative area of the parental apartment (F–I, M–P) is defined on the ground floor by a generous sequence of dining room, living room and fireplace parlor and on the upper story by the library, which is connected to the partially two-storied hall at the center of the house. The other spaces are clearly separated from this area, especially the study with separate access on the attic story. Likewise the second apartment for the adult children (E, J–L) is also subdivided in private and communal areas, although here the designations are less fixed.

The careful detailing serves dignified homeliness and longevity at the highest niveau of craftsmanship. The visible shell of the supporting structure consists of very bright white concrete. Windows and doors have been executed in architectural bronze, the last of this kind since the manufacturer has subsequently gone out of business. Oak parquet and Istrian limestone are used for the flooring with large-format slabs laid in sand. Selected walls are painted either in color or glossy white, which leads to surprising depth and light reflection effects. Such qualities, along with the suspenseful placement of windows and proportioning of the rooms, produce apartments with highly individualized layouts strongly relating the house to the lifestyle of its inhabitants.

Mitarbeit: Véronique Caviezel, Gian Andrea Serena
Landschaftsarchitektur: Appert Zwahlen Partner AG, Cham
Tragwerksplanung: ZPF Ingenieure AG, Basel
Fotos: Ruedi Walti

Staff: Véronique Caviezel, Gian Andrea Serena
Landscape Architecture: Appert Zwahlen Partner AG, Cham
Structural Engineering: ZPF Ingenieure AG, Basel
Photos: Ruedi Walti

Bericht zum Tragwerk
Helmuth Pauli

Das Generationenhaus in Binningen ist ein statisch sehr komplexes Gebäude, bestehend aus drei relevanten Tragelementen: dem teilweise beheizten Sockel (Untergeschoss), dem inneren warmen Tragwerk der Obergeschosse und der kalten Sichtbetonfassade. Diese drei Teile sind, wo notwendig, schalltechnisch und thermisch voneinander getrennt und doch miteinander zu einem ganzen Baukörper verbunden. Die spezielle Geometrie des Hauses mit den markanten Rücksprüngen der Fassade und den ebenfalls in Sichtbeton ausgeführten Untersichten der Auskragungen an der Nordwest- und Südwestseite machte das Trennen und Verbinden zu einer Herausforderung. Sie führte zu einer sehr aufwendigen Planung und erforderte eine intensive Zusammenarbeit mit den Architekten und der ausführenden Unternehmung.

Eine uns selbst auferlegte Anforderung bestand darin, eine fugenlose Sichtbetonfassade zu entwickeln, die sich infolge Temperaturwechsel unabhängig von der inneren Tragstruktur – die keinen Temperaturschwankungen ausgesetzt ist – ohne Zwängungen frei ausdehnen und zusammenziehen kann. Deshalb sind die im Dachgeschoss zurückversetzten Fassadenteile von der darunterliegenden Decke horizontal thermisch getrennt und örtlich auf Lagern abgestellt, welche die vertikalen und horizontalen Bewegungen zwängungsfrei zulassen.

Das Betonieren dieser komplexen Sichtbetonfassade erfolgte in Etappen, die durch die Architekten nach optischen Kriterien bestimmt und von uns zusammen mit dem Baumeister so modifiziert worden waren, dass ein hochwertiges Resultat der sichtbaren Oberfläche möglich wurde. Die Reihenfolge der einzelnen Betonieretappen wurde in Abhängigkeit zur inneren Tragstruktur festgelegt. Es sind zwei Systeme vorhanden, die sich sowohl hinsichtlich einer Optimierung der nutzbaren Flächen als auch aus statischen Gründen ergaben: Der klassische Aufbau mit innerer und äusserer Tragschale liegt nur bei der Westfassade vor; hier wurde zuerst die innere, dann die äussere Fassadenwand erstellt, was dem üblichen Betoniervorgang entspricht. Anstelle der inneren Wand wurden bei der Ostfassade Stahlstützen in die Dämmebene gestellt. An der Nord- und Südfassade sind jeweils beide Systeme vorhanden.

Die Fixierung der äusseren Fassadenwand an den Deckenstirnen erfolgte mittels nicht rostendem Betonrippenstahl, was die Aufnahme der Bewegungen garantierte. Je nachdem ob die Decke oder die Wand zuerst betoniert wurde, erfolgte der Einbau der Fassadenanker entweder an der inneren oder an der äusseren Konstruktion.

Die inneren Tragwände an der Westfassade sind notwendig, um die auskragenden Baukörper über dem Eingangsbereich im Nordwesten und dem gedeckten Sitzplatz im Südwesten jeweils im Erdgeschoss an die Längswände anzuhängen.

Die Grundstruktur der restlichen inneren Tragstruktur ist klar gegliedert und im Unter- und Erdgeschoss analog ausgeführt. Markant sind die zwei inneren Längswände und das Haupttreppenhaus mit dem Lift. Diese drei Tragelemente gehen mit Anpassungen bis ins Dachgeschoss durch und bilden auch die aussteifenden Elemente des Hauses. Die zusätzlichen Querwände in Ostwestrichtung sind als Abschluss der überhohen Räume erforderlich und in Beton ausgeführt. Damit wird eine Rissbildung und die unterschiedliche Färbung der Deckenstirn und der Wandfläche vermieden. Die Entwicklung solcher Details im Zusammenspiel mit dem übergeordneten Konzept des Tragwerks und der minutiösen Abstimmung des Betoniervorgangs machten den speziellen Reiz, aber auch die Herausforderung dieses Projekts aus.

Projektverantwortlicher:
Helmuth Pauli
Projektleiterin:
Heike Egli-Erhart

The Load-bearing Structure
Helmuth Pauli

Generational House in Binningen is a highly complex building structurally, which consists of three relevant load-bearing elements: the partially heated plinth (basement), the inner, warm load-bearing structure of the upper stories and the cold visible concrete façade. Wherever necessary, these three parts have been acoustically and thermally separated from each other and yet connected with each other into a cohesive volume. What made this separating and connecting a challenge is the special geometry of the house with its marked setbacks of the visible concrete façades and undersides of the cantilevers on the northwest and southwest sides, which are executed in the same material. This led to a very elaborate planning process requiring an intensive collaboration with the architects and executing contractors.

One of the tasks we set ourselves was to develop a seamless visible concrete façade, which in response to temperature fluctuations independent of the inner supporting structure – which is not exposed to temperature fluctuations – can freely expand and contract without restraining forces. To achieve this aim the set-back parts of the façade at the top floor are thermally separated horizontally from the underlying ceiling and locally placed on bearing supports that allow both vertical and horizontal movement without restraining forces.

The casting work for this complex visible concrete façade was executed in stages determined by the architects according to optical criteria and modified by us, together with the construction manager, so that a high-quality result of the visible surfaces could be achieved. The sequence of the individual casting stages was determined in correlation with the inner load-bearing structure. There are two systems in place that were employed to optimize usable surface as well as for structural reasons: the traditional system with inner and outer load-bearing panels is only present at the west façade; here first the inner and then the outer façade wall was erected, which corresponds to the usual casting process. For the east façade steel rebars were inserted into the insulation layer instead of the inner wall. Both systems were used for the north and south façades.

The fixation of the outer façade wall at the edges of the ceiling/floor slabs was achieved via corrosion-resistant concrete ribbed stainless steel rebar, which guarantees absorption of movement. Depending on whether the ceiling or wall had been cast first, the façade anchors were installed either at the inner or outer construction.

The inner load-bearing walls at the west façade are necessary in order to hang the cantilevered volumes over the northwest entrance area and the southwest sheltered seating area, each of which is attached on the ground floor to the longitudinal walls.

The basic structure of the rest of the interior load-bearing framework is clear-cut and executed in a similar way on both basement and ground levels. The two inner longitudinal walls and main stairwell with the elevator are striking. These three load-bearing elements extend all the way with adaptations to the uppermost story and also form the bracing elements of the house. The additional east-west transverse walls are necessary as the conclusion of the extra-high-ceilinged rooms and are executed in concrete. This prevents the formation of cracks and different coloration of the floor/ceiling slab edges and wall surfaces. The development of such details in interplay with the overriding concept of the load-bearing structure and meticulous coordination of the casting process constitute both the particular fascination and main challenge of this project.

Project Principal:
Helmuth Pauli
Project Manager:
Heike Egli-Erhart

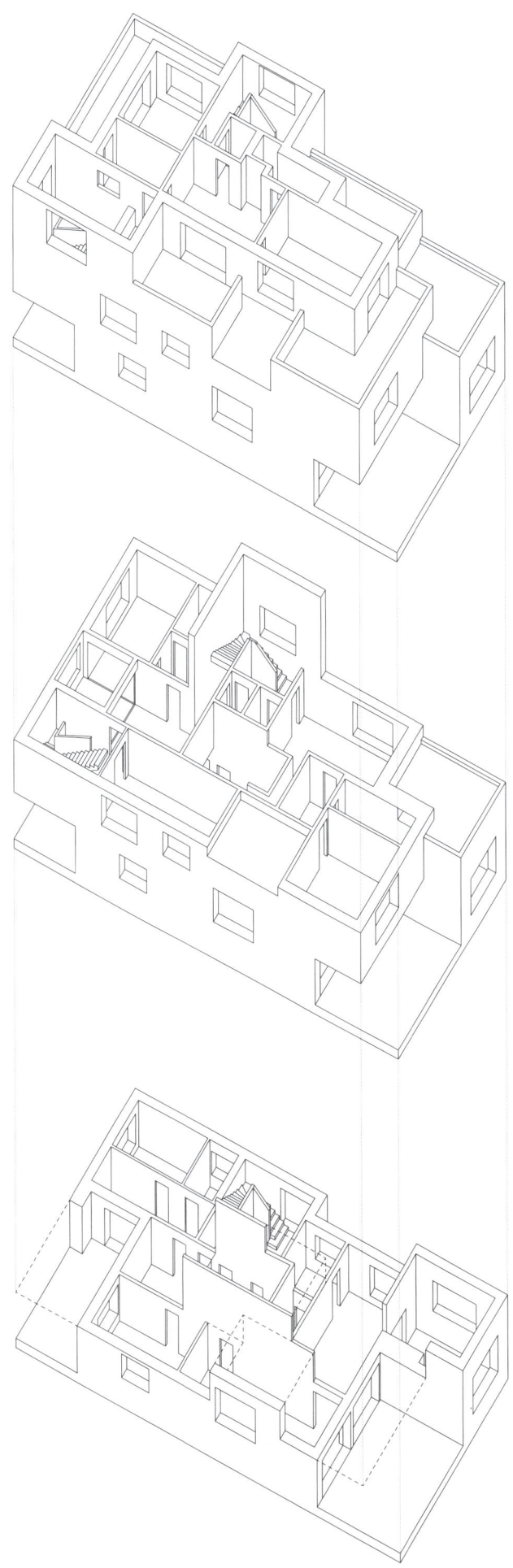

4F

4 G

4 H

4 J

4 K

4 L

4 M

4 N

4 O

4 P

Christoph Wieser
Herausgeber

Luca Selva Architekten
Acht Häuser und ein Pavillon

Wohnhaus für Künstler
　《 1–8
Doppelwohnhaus Bäumlihof
　《 9–14
Wohnhaus beim Wenkenpark
　《 15–20
Generationenhaus
　《 21–32
　　Bericht zum Tragwerk, Helmuth Pauli
　　← 26

　　Luca Selva:
　　Über die Verdichtung der Gedanken
　　beim Entwerfen
　　→ 34
　　Christoph Wieser:
　　Typen und Typologien
　　→ 36

Gartenpavillon
　↠ 49–52

　　Luca Selva im Gespräch
　　mit Daniel Buchner,
　　moderiert von Christoph Wieser
　　→ 53
　　Biografien, Mitarbeitende,
　　Werkverzeichnis, Impressum
　　→ 64

Wohnhaus mit Atelier
　↠ 69–74
Wohnhaus für Kunstsammler
　↠ 75–84
　　Der Stampflehmboden, Martin Rauch
　　↠ 78
Wohnhaus M.
　↠ 85–90
Haus H.
　↠ 91–96

Christoph Wieser
Editor

Luca Selva Architects
Eight Houses and a Pavilion

House for Artists
　《 1–8
Bäumlihof Duplex
　《 9–14
House at Wenkenpark
　《 15–20
Generational House
　《 21–32
　　The Load-bearing Structure, Helmuth Pauli
　　← 26

　　Luca Selva:
　　On the Condensation of Thoughts
　　in the Design Process
　　→ 34
　　Christoph Wieser:
　　Types and Typologies
　　→ 36

Garden Pavilion
　↠ 49–52

　　Luca Selva in Conversation
　　with Daniel Buchner,
　　moderated by Christoph Wieser
　　→ 53
　　Biographies, Staff Members,
　　Buildings, Projects, Imprint
　　→ 64

House with Studio
　↠ 69–74
House for Art Collectors
　↠ 75–84
　　Rammed Earth Floor, Martin Rauch
　　↠ 78
House M.
　↠ 85–90
House H.
　↠ 91–96

A
Nachwuchs-Campus FC Basel, Basel 2013
Youngster Campus FC Basel, Basel 2013

B
Wohnsiedlung Densa-Areal, Basel 2011
Densa-Areal Residential Complex, Basel 2011

C
Hofbebauung Hegenheimerstrasse, Basel 2011
Hegenheimerstrasse Backstreet Multiunit Residence, Basel 2011

D
Wohnhochhaus City Gate, Basel 2013
City Gate Residential High-Rise, Basel 2013

E
Schulhaus Erlenmatt, Basel 2017
Erlenmatt Schoolhouse, Basel 2017

F
Masterplan und Wohnbauten im KBB, Köln
Master Plan and Housing Complex at KBB, Cologne

Über die Verdichtung der Gedanken beim Entwerfen

On the Condensation of Thoughts in the Design Process

Uns interessiert das Genaue. In unseren Projekten suchen wir es als Umsetzung von Antworten auf präzise gestellte Fragen. So sind beispielsweise die Form des FCB-Campusgebäudes ←A oder die beiden klinkerverkleideten Solitärbauten für das Densa-Areal ←B genaue Antworten auf die Charakteristika der jeweiligen Orte. Auch die Hofbebauung an der Hegenheimerstrasse ←C bindet sich mit einer sorgfältig entwickelten Typologie in die Gesamtsituation ein, und das Wohnhochhaus City Gate ←D ist einer von vier geplanten Neubauten, die um einen hofartigen Binnenraum gruppiert sind. Derzeit beschäftigen uns etwa die Terrassentypologie des Schulhauses Erlenmatt ←E als Antwort für ein Primarschulhaus in städtischem Umfeld oder die insgesamt sieben Wohnbauten mit über 200 Wohnungen in einem denkmalgeschützten Industriekontext in Köln ←F.

      Ähnlich wie bei diesen grossen Projekten, ist es auch für die Programme der Einfamilienhäuser eine stete Herausforderung, dieses Genaue zu finden und zu entwickeln. Aber wie lässt es sich fassen? Wie wird ein Projekt «genau»? Dazu müssen zunächst die entsprechenden Fragen gestellt werden. Wer ist die Bauherrschaft, was sind ihre Programme, Träume und Unverträglichkeiten? Wie offen ist sie für den Entwicklungsprozess, und wie verhält sich ihre Entscheidungskultur dazu? Zudem: Was bedeutet der Ort für den Eingriff, was ist der Kontext, was sind die Vorschriften und was genau – und hier wird es spannend – ist die Erkenntnis aus diesen Fragestellungen, die zum Thema des Projektes werden könnte? Es geht in dieser Suche nicht darum, das Projekt als Summe der Erkenntnisse zu entwickeln, sondern eine Vielzahl architektonischer Gedanken in Form von Skizzen und Modellen – im Sinne Heinrich von Kleists[1] – kondensieren zu lassen, damit sie zum Leitmotiv werden. Kondensat verstehen wir als Verdichtungsprozess und Ausdruck des wechselnden Aggregatzustands im eigentlich physikalischen Sinn: Wir umkreisen diese Fragen mit den Mitteln der Architekten, suchen das Wesentliche, verwerfen Antworten, um erneut zu suchen und neue Fragen zu stellen auf der Basis der vorherigen Erkenntnisse, wiederholen den Prozess,

We are interested in exactness. In our projects we seek it as the transformation of answers to precisely posed questions. In this sense, e.g., the form of Youngster Campus FC Basel ←A or the two clinker-clad solitary buildings for Densa-Areal Residential Complex ←B are exact answers to the characteristics of the two different locations. Also Hegenheimerstrasse Backstreet Multiunit Residence ←C [*Hofbebauung*. In this case, "backstreet" refers to a *Hinterhof,* i.e., courtyard or backyard behind an existing block-style multiunit residential building] has been embedded into the overall situation through a carefully planned typology, and City Gate Residential High-Rise ←D is one of four planned new buildings that are grouped around an open space in the center to create a situation like an inner courtyard. At this time we are engaged with, e.g., the typologies of terraces at Erlenmatt Schoolhouse ←E as answer for a primary school in an urban context or Housing Complex in Cologne, a group of seven residential buildings with more than 200 apartments in a protected historical industrial context ←F.

      In a way similar to these larger projects, with the programs for single family houses finding and developing this exactness is a constant challenge. But how can it be grasped? How does a project become "exact"? First of all the commensurate questions have to be raised. Who is the client? What are their programs, dreams and intolerances? How open-minded is he or she to the development process, and how does his or her culture of decision-making react to the dynamic? Furthermore: What does the site mean for the intervention? What is the context? What regulations exist and what exactly – and here things get interesting – is the insight to be drawn from raising these questions that can become the theme of the project? The aim of this search is not to develop a project as sum of the findings but rather to allow the condensation – in the sense of Heinrich von Kleist[1] – of a multitude of architectonical thoughts in the form of sketches and models so that they become a leitmotif. We understand condensation as a process of densification and expression of changing states of aggregation in the

---

1   Bezugnehmend auf den Brief Heinrich von Kleists an R[ühle] v[on] L[ilienstern]: «Über die allmähliche Verfertigung der Gedanken beim Reden» (ca. 1806), in: Heinrich von Kleist, *Sämtliche Werke und Briefe in vier Bänden*, 3. Bd., hg. von Helmut Sembdner, München/Wien 1982, S. 319–324.

1   This refers to a letter from Heinrich von Kleist to R[ühle] v[on] L[ilienstern]: "Über die allmähliche Verfertigung der Gedanken beim Reden" (c. 1806), in: Heinrich von Kleist, *Sämtliche Werke und Briefe in vier Bänden*, vol. 3, ed. by Helmut Sembdner (Munich/Vienna 1982), 319–324. In English: "On the Gradual Construction of Thought by Speech," translated by Michael Hamburger, in: *German Life and Letters* 5/1 (1951): 42–46.

Über die Verdichtung der Gedanken beim Entwerfen
Luca Selva

bis wir ein tragfähiges Thema für den Entwurf kondensiert haben.

In den Häusern, die in diesem Band dokumentiert sind, zeigt sich eine grosse Bandbreite solcher Themen oder Leitmotive. Die aus ihnen entstandenen Architekturen sind sehr unterschiedlich, in einem gewissen Sinn sehr personalisiert; sie alle verbindet jedoch das Genaue, das sich einmal in Form einer dem Kontext verpflichteten Materialisierung, einmal in der Typologie, einmal in der Umsetzung der Programme oder in der Gebäudeform respektive dem Gebäudeschnitt findet. Dabei zeigt eine chronologische Betrachtung, dass sich die materialgebundenen Fragestellungen, wie beispielsweise im Doppelwohnhaus Bäumlihof «9, hin zu räumlich-typologischen Aspekten verschoben haben, wie sie im Haus für Künstler «1 oder im neuesten Haus H. in Riehen »91 zu finden sind. Die Raumfiguren werden komplexer und stärker wahrnehmbar durch die Präzisierung der eingesetzten Materialien. Allen Häusern gemeinsam ist jedoch der entwerferische Prozess, in dem die Bauherrschaft eine wichtige Rolle spielt und aktiv in die Entwicklung miteinbezogen wird. Wir haben – im Sinne eines Couturier – ihr Mass genommen, haben ihnen genaue Fragen gestellt und die Antworten in den Entwicklungsprozess des Projektes aufgenommen. So entstanden sehr individuelle Masskonfektionen, kein Prêt-à-porter. Alle Häuser tragen diese Verdichtung der Gedanken in sich, die zu dem «Genauen» führen, das uns im Umgang mit Architektur so sehr interessiert.

On the Condensation of Thoughts in the Design Process
Luca Selva

actual physical sense: we circle these questions with the means of architects, seek the essentials, discard answers in order to newly search to raise new questions on the basis of earlier findings and then repeat the process until we have condensed a sturdy and potent theme for carrying through the design process.

The houses that have been documented in this publication demonstrate a broad spectrum of such themes or leitmotifs. The resulting architectures are very different, in a certain sense highly personalized; but they are all joined by exactness, which sometimes is to be found in the context-based materialization, sometimes in the typology, sometimes in the implementation of the program or in the building's form relative to its section. Thereby considering these projects chronologically shows that material-related questions, e.g., Bäumlihof Duplex «9, have given way to spatial-typological aspects, as evidenced by House for Artists «1 or most recently by House H. in Riehen »91. The spatial figures have become more complex and powerfully perceptible through the precision of the execution materials. What all houses have in common, however, is the design process in which clients play an important role and are actively involved in the development. We have – in the sense of a *couturier* – taken their measurements, have asked them precise questions and integrated the answers into the development process of the project. The result is highly individualized custom-made, not prêt-à-porter. All of the houses bear this condensation of thoughts that leads to the "exactness" which interests us so much in our engagement with architecture.

Types and Typologies

Christoph Wieser

Designing a single family house is arguably the most individualized task an architect can face. Rather than being corporate entities, the clients are private persons with their own, sometimes unconventional ideas of housing. What's expected is a building tailored to personal needs: a custom-made suit, not a mass-produced garment. In his groundbreaking book *Der moderne Zweckbau* (1926) [The Modern Functional Building], which offers a thorough, comprehensive overview of the aims and tendencies of Modern Architecture, Adolf Behne describes the difference between Rationalism and Functionalism as follows: "As the functionalist looks for the greatest possible adaptation to the most specialized purpose, so the rationalist looks for the most appropriate solution for many cases. The former wants what is absolutely fitting and unique for the particular case, the latter wants what is most fitting for general need, the norm."[1] According to Behne these different attitudes also correspond to the disparate interpretations of the term "purpose": "The functionalist prefers to exaggerate the purpose to the point of making it unique and momentary (a house for each function!), but the rationalist takes the purpose broadly and generally as readiness for many cases, simply because he gives thought to the enduring qualities of buildings, which perhaps see many generations with changing requirements and therefore cannot live without — leeway."[2]

Individualized Case, Character and Type

Behne's characterization of functionalists and rationalists is also interesting beyond its historical relevance, namely with respect to the fundamental nature of his proposition. In a pointed way he describes different possibilities of how a spatial program can be rendered in a building. In other words this concerns the question of whether the house is considered as the most individualized expression of the inhabitants or rather as the type, which gives form to generalized concepts. Staying with the same image that Behne uses elsewhere, single family houses naturally tend to be "gloves" [rather than "mittens"]. This not only has to do with the personified client but also with the clear-cut, overseeable program, which suggests

---

[1] Adolf Behne, *The Modern Functional Building*, trans. by Michael Robinson (Santa Monica, CA 1996), 138. Orig.: *Der moderne Zweckbau* (Munich / Vienna / Berlin 1926), 62.

[2] Ibid.

an individualized design approach. All projects of Luca Selva Architects, but particularly the residential buildings for one or two parties, are in the best sense such "gloves": while relating to the program, site, energy requirements and financial means and needs of the client, they keep their own identity. The focus on specific and not on general aspects of the architectural task is already demonstrated with some residential buildings by their designations: House for Art Collectors ≫75, Generational House ≪21 or House with Studio ≫69.

At the same time all the dwellings point to something beyond themselves. On the one hand, they are "mittens" in the sense that they have originated as part of the firm's design research process, on the basis of themes that prove to be fruitful, are further developed and re-applied in an adapted form. On the other hand, the projects are always modifications of basic architectonic types so that they can be read as representatives of primary categories. The classification of the dwellings can ensue according, e.g., to program (House for Art Collectors ≫75, Garden Pavilion ≫49), ground plan typology (house with inner courtyard, angle), spatial character (one room house, chambering) or geometrical features (orthogonal or polygonal articulation). With each house the extent to which one or more of the aforementioned or further categories are accentuated varies in degree. This creates ambiguity that lends depth and substance to the projects. Furthermore the great variety in formal appearance reflects a characteristic trait of the type, whose *Gestalt,* in contrast to the model's and in terms of potential design development, is open.

Antoine Chrysostôme Quatremère de Quincy (1755–1849), French art historian and notable early theoretician of typology, writes about this topic: "'Type' refers less to the image of a thing to be copied or completely imitated than an idea which should serve as the rule for the model.[...] The artistic model, on the other hand, is an object that has to be reproduced as it is. In contrast, the type is something on the basis of which works can be designed that do not appear similar to each other at all. With the model everything is precisely prespecified; with the type everything remains more or less undefined."[3] What is fascinating about the type is exactly its formal capability of development in combination with the prefixation of decisive characteristics that contain the, so to speak, genetic code of the building. A type predetermines ordering principles that can be differently weighed and interpreted depending on the situation.

[3] English translation from the German citation in: Wolfgang Kemp, *Architektur analysieren* (Munich 2009), 331.

Code des Gebäudes beinhalten. Ein Typ gibt Ordnungen vor, die aber je nach Situation unterschiedlich gewichtet und interpretiert werden können.

So wird beispielsweise beim Wohnhaus am Wenkenpark «15, wo Luca Selva Architekten das Prinzip des Einraumhauses zum ersten Mal angewendet haben, dieser Typus räumlich und formal völlig anders umgesetzt als beim Wohnhaus mit Atelier in Muttenz. Zudem handelt es sich beim zweiten nicht um einen reinen Typ: die Bezeichnung als Einraumhaus bezieht sich auf den offen fliessenden Bereich der repräsentativen Räume von der Eingangshalle über die Wohn- und Essräume bis zur Loggia, die dem Haus seinen spezifischen Charakter verleihen. Damit ist explizit der räumliche Charakter gemeint, nicht der formale, atmosphärische oder gar stilistische, wie er beim Begriff des *caractère* im Vordergrund steht, der dem Typus vorranging und inhaltich eng mit diesem verwandt ist. Germain Boffrand forderte 1734: «Jedes Haus soll vom Aussenbau bis zur Einrichtung den Charakter seines Erbauers ausdrücken und ablesbar machen.»[4] Diese Forderung hatte eine weitreichende, zumindest theoretische Ausdifferenzung zur Folge. Jacques-François Blondel zählt in seinem *Cours d'architecture* von 1766 insgesamt 38 verschiedene Charaktere auf, die von viril, elegant, ländlich bis zu geheimnisvoll und frivol reichen.[5] Bei den Wohnhäusern von Luca Selva Architekten bezieht sich die typologische beziehungsweise «charaktermässige» Ausbildung der Bauten in erster Linie auf architektonisch-räumliche Themen. Diese stehen aber nicht im luftleeren Raum, sondern spiegeln gesellschaftliche Konventionen wider, ebenso wie der Einsatz bestimmter Materialien – Bronzefenster, massive Holzriemenböden oder ein besonders delikater Verputz – den hohen Ansprüchen der privaten Bauherrschaften Ausdruck verleiht.

Raumkonfigurationen

Die Beziehung zwischen den einzelnen Räumen der Wohnhäuser von Luca Selva Architekten folgt unterschiedlichen Prinzipien. Das Einraumhaus wurde bereits erwähnt; dazu kommen mehr oder weniger stark gekammerte Grundrisse. Bezüglich der vertikalen Organisation gibt es einige wenige Projekte, die geschossweise gegliedert sind, wie das Doppelwohnhaus Bäumlihof «9. In der Regel jedoch fungieren mehrgeschossige Räume als Bindeglieder zwischen den Etagen – beim Wohnhaus M.→A ist es eine rund neun Meter hohe Treppenhalle – oder die Häuser verfügen gar über einen Loos'schen Raumplan.

So, for instance, with House at Wenkenpark «15, where Luca Selva Architects employs the principle of the one room house for the first time, this type is spatially and formally rendered in a completely different way than at House with Studio in Muttenz. Moreover, the latter does not constitute a pure type: its categorization as one room house refers to the openly flowing area of the representative spaces extending from the foyer across the living and dining rooms to the loggia, which lend the house its specific character. What is explicitly meant thereby is the spatial character, not the formal, not the atmospheric or especially not the stylistic, as is foregrounded by the term *caractère*, which preceded the notion of the type and is closely related to it in meaning. In 1734 Germain Boffrand claims: "Every house should express and make the character of its master builder readable from the exterior structure to the interior furnishings."[4] This stipulation led to a wide-ranging especially theoretical nuancing. In his *Cours d'architecture* (1766) Jacques-François Blondel lists a total of 38 different characters ranging from virile, elegant and rural to mysterious and frivolous.[5] With the residential buildings by Luca Selva Architects the typological, i.e., "character-related" genesis of the buildings mainly refers to architectonic-spatial themes. However, these do not exist in a vacuum but reflect societal conventions as well as the use of certain materials – bronze windows, solid wood plank flooring or particularly delicate plasterwork – expressing the high standards of the private clients.

Configurations of Space

The relationship between the individual spaces of the dwellings by Luca Selva Architects follows different principles. The one room house has already been mentioned; in addition, there are more or less strongly chambered ground plans. In terms of the vertical organization there are a few projects that are divided by story, such as Bäumlihof Duplex «9. As a rule, however, multi-story spaces function as linking elements between the levels – in House M. →A there is an approximately nine-meter-high stairway hall – or the dwellings even possess a Loosian *Raumplan*. [Trans. note: This spatial concept aims to avoid separated floors and structures space in a sequence of stepped areas with different ceiling heights according to the function of the room.]

The most complex example of this kind is undoubtedly Generational House «21 in Binningen. Underlying the three-story cubically

---

4 Zitiert nach: ebd., S. 327.

5 Vgl. ebd.

4 Cited from: ibid., 327.

5 Cf. ibid.

A
Wohnhaus M., Binningen 2013
House M., Binningen 2013

B
Generationenhaus, Binningen 2013
Generational House, Binningen 2013

C
Wohnhaus beim Wenkenpark, Riehen 2004
House at Wenkenpark, Riehen 2004

D
Josef Frank, Villa Wehtje, Falsterbo 1935
Villa Wehtje, Arch.: Josef Frank, Falsterbo 1935

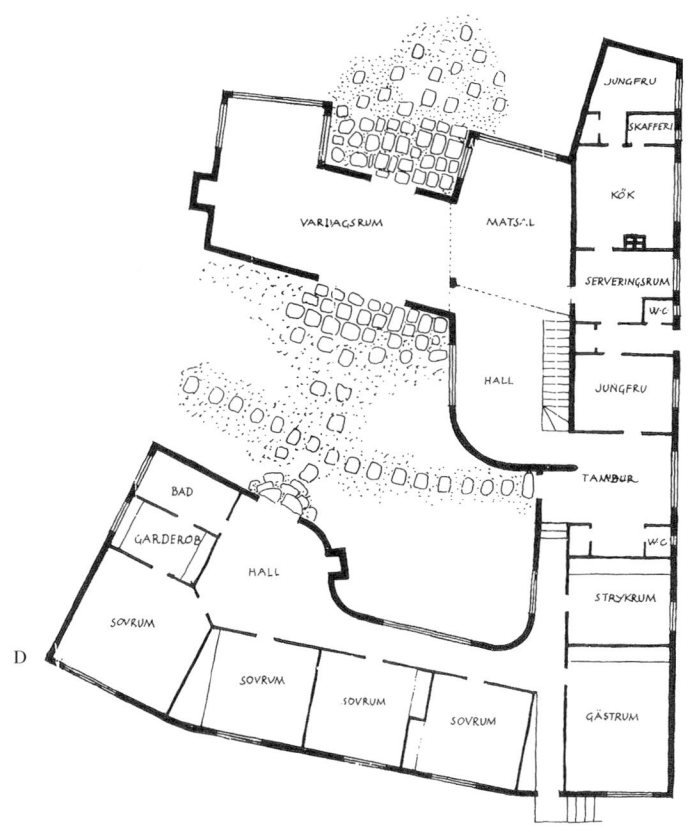

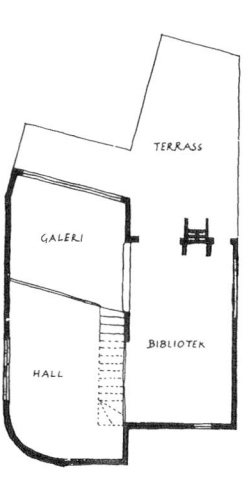

| Typen und Typologien | Raumkonfigurationen | Types and Typologies | Configurations of Space |

Das komplexeste Beispiel dieser Art ist zweifellos das Generationenhaus in Binningen «21. Dem dreigeschossigen, kubisch gegliederten Volumen liegt eine kammerartige Struktur zugrunde, die zwei Wohnungen unterschiedlicher Ausprägung miteinander verschränkt. Dank des klaren, aber nicht modularen Systems können Räume unterschiedlicher Höhe und horizontaler Ausdehnung zu einem vielfältigen, puzzleartigen Ganzen gefügt werden. Der deutsche Philosoph Otto Friedrich Bollnow hat in seinem Buch *Mensch und Raum* (1963) auf die Diskrepanz zwischen dem geometrisch gegebenen und dem von den Bewohnern erlebten Raum hingewiesen.[6]

Beim Generationenhaus ←B wird dieser Unterschied besonders deutlich: Beide Wohnungen folgen ihrer eigenen Logik, haben Zimmer in alle vier Himmelsrichtungen und auf allen drei Geschossen. Dabei wechselt man beim Durchschreiten mehrmals die Richtung und verliert, gerade weil die Räume als zwar grosszügig miteinander verbundene, aber eigenständige Zimmer ausgebildet sind, unweigerlich das Gefühl für den (geometrischen) Gesamtzusammenhang. Exemplarisch zeigt sich dies im Studierzimmer der Hauptwohnung, das über eine eigene Treppe erschlossen ist und im Attikageschoss als einsame Klause, entrückt vom Rest der Wohnung, erfahren wird. Konzeptionell völlig anders ist die Raumplan-Idee beim Haus H. ↠91 umgesetzt. Dort bildet das räumlich «atmende» Treppenhaus das Rückgrat des Gebäudes mit dem Cheminée als atmosphärischem Zentrum. Die sich um den Kern windenden Geschosse sind in eine Abfolge von Stufen und Podesten aufgeteilt, von denen aus die Räume erschlossen werden. Dank dieser Aufsplittung wird die Zusammengehörigkeit der Ebenen trotz Einteilung des Grundrisses in einzelne Zimmer betont.

Beim Typ des Einraumhauses arbeiten Luca Selva Architekten auf differenzierte Weise mit Zonierungen des fliessenden Raumes: in der Horizontalen mittels Einschnürungen und Ausweitungen sowie einer präzisen Setzung der Öffnungen, in der Vertikalen mittels unterschiedlichen Raumhöhen und einer Abstufung der Ebenen. Auch ohne Türen werden auf diese Weise Schwellen ausgebildet, die hierarchisierend wirken. Ganz so wie bei der Villa Wehtje (1935) ←D von Josef Frank im südschwedischen Falsterbo. Dort ist der Zugang in die privaten Gemächer allein mit zwei Treppenstufen vom Eingangsbereich abgetrennt, wogegen der Auftakt in den repräsentativen Wohnflügel schwellenlos und mit einer doppelgeschossigen Halle erfolgt. Gerade wegen ihrer

articulated volumes is a chamber-like structure which interlinks two differently configured apartments. The clear but non-modular system serves in fusing rooms of differing heights and horizontal dimensions into a multifaceted, puzzle-like whole. In his book *Mensch und Raum* (1963) [Human Space] the German philosopher Otto Friedrich Bollnow has pointed out the discrepancy between mathematically/geometrically-prescribed and inhabitant-experienced space.[6]

This discrepancy becomes especially obvious in Generational House: both apartments follow their own logic and have rooms extending in all four directions and on all three stories. Pacing through the building means changing directions several times and inevitably losing any sense of the overall (geometrical) cohesiveness. Exactly this happens because although the spaces are generously interconnected, they are also articulated as separate rooms. Representing this in an exemplary way is the study of the main apartment, which is accessible via its own staircase and experienced as a retreat on the attic story removed from the rest of the apartment. The *Raumplan* idea is realized in a completely different way conceptually in House H. ↠91. There the spatially "breathing" stairwell forms the backbone of the building with a fireplace as atmospheric center. Winding around the core, the stories are articulated as a series of steps and landings from which the spaces are accessible. This fragmentation serves to emphasize the cohesiveness of the levels despite the segmentation of the ground plan into individual rooms.

Working with the type of the one room house in a very particular way, Luca Selva Architects uses zoning of the flowing space: horizontally through constriction and expansion as well as meticulous placement of openings; and vertically through different spatial heights and terracing of the levels. Even without doors in this way thresholds are formed that function hierarchically, just as at Villa Wehtje (1935) ←D by Josef Frank in Falsterbo in southern Sweden. There the entrance to the private chambers is divided from the entrance area solely by two stairsteps, whereas the prelude to the representative residential wing proceeds without any threshold and via a two-story hall. Precisely because of their spatial articulation in a sequence of differently proportioned spaces and zones, the one room houses by Luca Selva Architects differ from the loft type and despite their space-consuming openness maintain a homeliness that is rooted in the bourgeois tradition but has been reinterpreted in a contemporary way.

6 Bollnow, Otto Friedrich, *Mensch und Raum*, 6. Aufl., Stuttgart/Berlin/Köln 1990, S. 194.

6 Otto Friedrich Bollnow, *Mensch und Raum*, 6th edition (Stuttgart/Berlin/Cologne 1990), 194. English edition: *Human Space*, translated by Christine Shuttleworth, edited by Joseph Kohlmaier (London 2011).

| Typen und Typologien | Innen und aussen | Types and Typologies | Inside and Outside |

räumlichen Differenzierung in eine Abfolge unterschiedlich proportionierter Räume und Zonen unterscheiden sich die Einraumhäuser von Luca Selva Architekten vom Typus des Lofts und behalten trotz raumgreifender Offenheit eine in der bürgerlichen Tradition verankerte, aber zeitgemäss interpretierte Wohnlichkeit bei.

Innen und aussen

Wohnlichkeit wird auch mit der Ausbildung der Öffnungen erreicht, die in den meisten Fällen als Fenster, nicht in Glas aufgelöste Wandflächen in Erscheinung treten. Obwohl die Raumgefüge im Innern eine hohe Durchlässigkeit aufweisen und über grosszügige Öffnungen verfügen, wirken die Räume gefasst. Dazu nochmals Bollnow: «Zunächst muss der Wohnraum den Eindruck der Abgeschlossenheit machen. Wenn es die Aufgabe des Hauses ist, dem Menschen Zuflucht vor der Aussenwelt zu geben, dann muss dies auch in der Art des Wohnraums zum Ausdruck kommen. In einem Flur kann man sich nicht behaglich aufhalten. Auch zu grosse Fenster oder ganze Glaswände, die den Raum in die Aussenwelt hinein öffnen, unterdrücken die Wohnlichkeit des Raums.»[7] Hier zeigt sich, wie bei Behne, eine gewisse Zeitgebundenheit der Aussage. Bollnows Buch datiert von 1963; der Öffnungsanteil als Gradmesser von Behaglichkeit und Wohnlichkeit ist keine fixe Grösse, wohl aber ein Indikator.

    Luca Selva Architekten arbeiten sehr bewusst mit traditionellen und innovativen Aspekten, um den gewünschten Charakter zu erzeugen, sei es bei der Verwendung von Materialien, bezüglich räumlicher Dispositionen oder in der Ausbildung einzelner Elemente. Bei den Öffnungen zeigt sich dies besonders deutlich. Traditionellerweise sind die Fenster im Aussenwandquerschnitt in etwa mittig angeordnet, was in konstruktiver und bauphysikalischer Hinsicht sinnvoll ist und beim Wohnhaus am Wenkenpark ←C eine zeitgemässe Umsetzung findet. Die Öffnungen liegen in der Dämmebene zwischen der inneren, tragenden, und der äusseren Schale in Klinker. Sie fungieren somit bautechnisch, aber auch architektonisch als klassische Bindeglieder zwischen innen und aussen: Indem die Fenster samt Leibungen in Eiche ausgeführt sind, wie die Böden und alle übrigen Schreinerarbeiten, erscheinen sie dem Innenraum zugehörig. Über den Holzton verbinden sie sich aber auch mit dem Klinker, sodass sie von aussen betrachtet zur Hülle gezählt werden können.

Inside and Outside

Homeliness is also achieved through the articulation of openings, which in most cases appear as windows rather than wall surfaces completely dissolved in glass. Although the spatial arrangements in the interior exhibit a high degree of permeability and are equipped with generous openings, the spaces appear contained. Referring again to Bollnow: "To start with, the dwelling space must give the impression of seclusion. If it is the task of a house to provide a refuge from the outside world, this must also find expression in the nature of the dwelling space. One cannot comfortably spend time in an entrance hall. Overlarge windows and walls made entirely of glass, which open the space to the outside world, suppress the homeliness of the space."[7] As with Behne's claim, the statement here is to some extent dated. Bollnow's book is from 1963: the proportion of openings as a measure of comfort and homeliness is not a fixed ratio but rather an indicator.

    Luca Selva Architects works very consciously with traditional and innovative aspects to create the desired character, be it through the use of materials, in terms of spatial disposition or through the articulation of individual elements. This is especially apparent with the openings. Traditionally, as considered in the cross section of the exterior wall, windows are approximately centered, which makes sense from a constructive and structural point of view and has been implemented in a contemporary way in House at Wenkenpark ←C. The openings lie in the insulation layer between the inner load-bearing wall and outer clinker shell. As a result they not only function structurally but also architectonically as classical elements connecting inside and outside: since the windows including the scuncheons, i.e., the inside face of the window frames, are executed in oak, like the floors and all other carpentry work, they seem to belong to the interior. The hue of the wood, however, also connects them to the clinker so that from outside they could be viewed as belonging to the hull.

    Despite the similar position in the cross section of the exterior wall, the intermediary moment plays a subordinate role in Generational House ←B. Here the bronze windows are theatrically staged as valuable, independent elements; they are ornaments in the walls that frame the view rather than connective elements joining inside and outside. The pictorial effect of the window is most clearly expressed in House for Art Collectors ≫75

---

7   Ebd., S. 150.

7   Ibid., 143.
In the German edition, 150.

| Typen und Typologien | Innen und aussen | Types and Typologies | Inside and Outside |

Das vermittelnde Moment spielt beim Generationenhaus ←B trotz ähnlicher Lage im Mauerquerschnitt eine untergeordnete Rolle. Hier werden die Bronzefenster als hochwertige, eigenständige Elemente inszeniert; sie sind eher Schmuckstücke der Wände, die die Aussicht rahmen, denn Bindeglieder zwischen innen und aussen. Die bildhafte Wirkung der Fenster kommt im Wohnhaus für Kunstsammler »75 in der Symbiose von Kunstwerken und Öffnungen am deutlichsten zum Ausdruck. Indem die Fenster innenbündig angeschlagen und wie die Wände weiss gestrichen sind, erscheint die Landschaft wie eine Fotografie. Präzise kadriert vom nahezu unsichtbaren Fensterrahmen, «fällt» die Umgebung in den Innenraum ein. Obwohl sie dadurch im Innern sehr präsent ist, in beinahe hyperrealistischer Art, entsteht eine Distanz zur Aussenwelt, weil das vermittelnde Element der Leibung fehlt. Man fühlt sich als Beobachter, nicht als Teilnehmer an der Welt da draussen. Das liegt auch daran, dass die Öffnungen als Festverglasungen ausgebildet sind, in der Regel mit einem schmalen, glaslosen Lüftungsflügel daneben.

Diese Kombination samt innenbündigem Anschlag, der farblichen Verschmelzung von Wand und Fensterrahmen sowie den meist liegenden, eleganten Proportionen hat sich im Lauf der letzten Jahre zu einem Kennzeichen der Wohnhäuser von Luca Selva Architekten entwickelt. Dazu gehört auch die sorgfältig austarierte Gestaltung der Fassaden. Bei insgesamt asymmetrischer Gliederung werden an bestimmten Stellen über die Setzung der Fenster Lokalsymmetrien gebildet. Das verleiht den Häusern eine Präsenz, wie man sie von Alvaro Sizas Bauten kennt, und sie «erdet» die von aussen oft frei komponiert erscheinenden Fassaden.

Einen unmittelbaren Bezug zum Garten stellen teils grossformatige Schiebetüren her, etwa beim Doppelwohnhaus Bäumlihof «9 oder dem Wohnhaus beim Wenkenpark «15. Dennoch bleibt die Grenze zwischen innen und aussen spürbar, weil die Öffnungen nie raumhoch, sondern als grosse Zäsuren in den Wandflächen ausgebildet sind. Sogar beim Wohnhaus für Künstler «1 sind die Wände gegen den Innenhof nicht bis unter das offene, schräge Dach, sondern nur bis auf die Höhe der umlaufenden Traufe in Glas aufgelöst. Dadurch behält das Wohngeschoss trotz aller Offenheit nach innen eine wohltuende räumliche Fassung.

Hier zeigt sich auf exemplarische Weise ein weiteres Thema, das die Wohnbauten von Luca Selva Architekten auszeichnet: der

in the symbiosis of artworks and openings. By mounting the windows flush with the inner wall and painting them white like the walls, the landscape looks like a photograph. Precisely framed by the almost invisible window frame, the surroundings "invade" the interior space. Although the landscape is thereby very present in the interior in a nearly hyperrealistic way, distance to the outer world emerges because of the lack of the mediating element of the scuncheon. One feels like a viewer rather than participant in the world outside. This is also because the openings are articulated as fixed glazing, as a rule with a small, non-glazed ventilation shutter at the side.

This combination — including the flush mounting at the interior wall, merging of wall and window frames through color as well as the mostly horizontal, elegant proportions — has become one of the trademarks of residential buildings designed by Luca Selva Architects over the past few years. Also to be mentioned here is the carefully balanced design of the façade. Generally employing asymmetric articulation, through the positioning of windows at certain locations local symmetries are formed, recalling the work of Alvaro Siza and "grounding" the façades which often from the outside appear to be freely composed.

An immediate relationship to the garden is created by (partially) large-format sliding doors, e.g., at Bäumlihof Duplex «9 or House at Wenkenpark «15. Nevertheless the boundary between inside and outside remains discernable because the openings never extend the full room height but are designed as large incisions in the wall surface. Even in House for Artists «1 the walls facing the inner courtyard are not dissolved in glass up to the underside of the open slanted roof but rather only up to the height of the encasing eaves. This ensures that the residential story maintains a soothing spatial closure towards the interior despite all the openness.

Here another theme that is demonstrated in Luca Selva Architects' residential buildings becomes evident in an exemplary way: "self-referential" views within the interior often combined with surprising through-views. In House M. the horseshoe-shaped volumetric form in combination with precisely positioned openings enable a view from the dining area through the three-sided glazed interior courtyard into the opposite spaces and beyond to outside. Depending on the conditions of lighting and time of day, this multi-faceted layering of space can be spectacularly accentuated or only barely noticeable and calls to

mind Baroque interiors and their virtuoso play with such phenomena.

To elaborate on this, a final citation from Bollnow: "The limits of parts of space that were clearly delineated in the Renaissance are veiled by overlapping sculptural decoration, the bordering wall becomes invisible to the observer, because he feels confused by a tangle of projecting and retreating parts, by one view and another, so that he finally no longer knows, and no longer asks, whether anything solid is still to be found behind all these views." [8] While in the Baroque the aim was to create a sense of infinity, in Luca Selva Architects' buildings the treatment of self-referential views in the interior can be interpreted as a reaction to the mainly heterogeneous environment: By turning the house's own rooms into a vis-à-vis and also by constituting selective views into the surroundings as prefigured frames of visual reference, the domestic world that is typically limited by the size of the surface area of its plot experiences unexpected expansion and spaciousness. The effect is enhanced by the deployment of polygonal spaces whose dimensions are much more difficult to gauge than the perpendicular.

Orthogonal versus Polygonal Spaces

Along with classical perpendicularity, complex geometries of different forms play an important role in the works of Luca Selva Architects, particularly in the single family houses. From House for Artists →G to House M. ⇾85, where nearly all of the spaces feature oblique angles, over the years the architects have accumulated a multitude of experiences with the effects of polygonal spaces. House for Artists is the architects' first and so far only building that deviates from the right angle in ground plan as well as section; in all subsequent projects obliqueness has been limited to the ground plan.

In Lupsingen the reason for the multiple pitches of the roof lies in the building regulations that stipulate a hip or gable roof. Luca Selva Architects' decision to use a hip roof but replacing its ridge with an inner courtyard results in the interior in intriguing roof spans, which when viewed from the underside reveal folds and respectively ascending and descending heights of the spaces. In addition, deliberately omitting a canopy produces a sharp-edged volume and geometrically challenging corner situations requiring highly skilled craftsmanship for the execution.

House with Studio ←1 is an illustrative example of the effect of a polygonal ground plan

---

8 Ibid., 85.
In the German edition, 87.

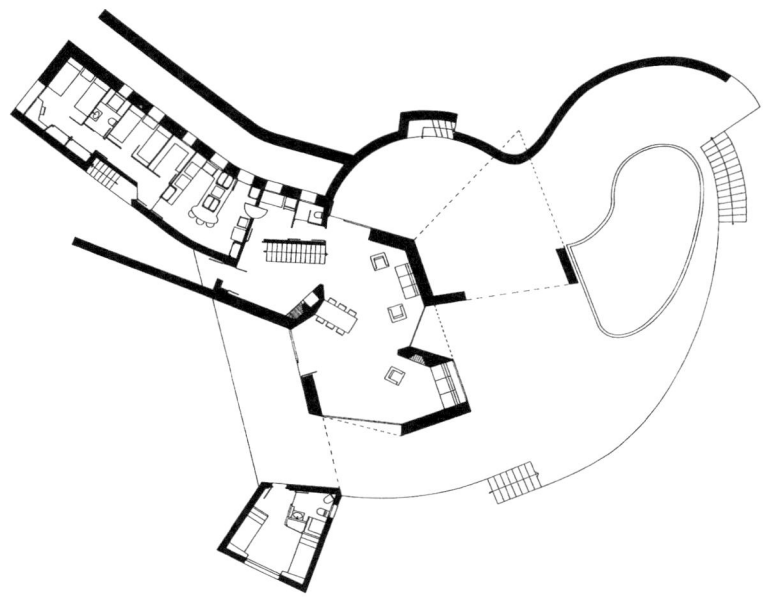
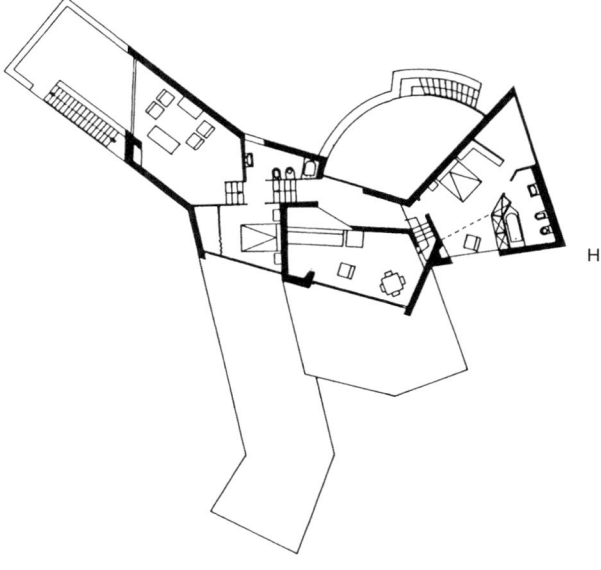

F
Wohnhaus für Kunstsammler, Binningen 2008
House for Art Collectors, Binningen 2008

G
Wohnhaus für Künstler, Lupsingen 2005
House for Artists, Lupsingen 2005

H
José Antonio Coderch, Wohnhaus Ugalde in Caldes d'Estrac, Barcelona 1952
House Ugalde in Caldes d'Estrac, Arch.: José Antonio Coderch, Barcelona 1952

I
Wohnhaus mit Atelier, Muttenz 2012
House with Studio, Muttenz 2012

ein Walm- oder Satteldach vorschreibt. Indem sich Luca Selva Architekten für ein Walmdach entschieden, dessen First jedoch durch einen Innenhof ersetzten, ergibt sich im Innern eine spannende Dachuntersicht mit Faltungen und ansteigenden beziehungsweise sich verringernden Raumhöhen. Zudem erzeugt der Verzicht auf ein Vordach ein scharfkantiges Volumen und geometrisch herausfordernde Ecksituationen, die ein hohes handwerkliches Können voraussetzten.

Beim Wohnhaus mit Atelier ←1 zeigt sich exemplarisch die Wirkungsweise eines polygonalen Grundrisses im Vergleich zu einem rechteckigen. Während beim Rechteck die Raumkanten eine deutliche Zäsur darstellen, unterstreichen stumpfe Winkel die Zusammengehörigkeit der Fassadenflächen, respektive die Kontinuität der Räume im Innern. Damit wird sowohl die Einheit des Gebäudekörpers gestärkt als auch dem Prinzip des Einraumhauses optimal entsprochen: Polygonale Geometrien unterstreichen das «fliessende» Element der Raumfolge, die Übergänge werden «weicher», ohne dass es dazu einer organischen Form bedürfte. Josef Frank hat bei der bereits erwähnten Villa Wehtje ←D schiefwinklige, orthogonale und organische Formen kombiniert. 1931 beschrieb er die Vorzüge polygonaler Räume aus seiner Sicht: «Der rechtwinklige Wohnraum eignet sich am wenigsten gut zum Wohnen; er ist als Möbelmagazin sehr praktisch, ansonsten jedoch zu nichts nütze. Ich glaube, dass man einen besser geeigneten Raum erhält, wenn man aufs Geratewohl ein Polygon mit rechten oder schiefen Winkeln zeichnet, als es ein regelmässig rechtwinkliger ist. In Dachräumen half der Zufall mit, so dass solche fast immer angenehm und persönlich wirken.»[9]

Frank hat den Zufall als Gestaltungsmittel in seinem späten Text «Akzidentismus» (1958) zum Programm erhoben, um der Eintönigkeit und Sterilität rein funktional bedingter Formgebung etwas entgegenzusetzen. Dabei zielte er nicht auf Willkürlichkeit, sondern auf einen massvollen Grad an Freiheit: «Was wir brauchen ist eine weit grössere Elastizität, aber keine starren Formgesetze […].»[10] Diese Art von Elastizität, auf spezifische Anforderungen mit spezifischen Formen zu antworten, findet in polygonalen Räumen ihren kongenialen Ausdruck. Zumindest suggerieren dies schiefwinklige Geometrien. Sie wirken – ob es tatsächlich zutrifft oder nicht – subjektiver als rechtwinklige Räume. In unserer technisierten Welt steht das Orthogonale für Rationalität; dem Polygonalen dagegen haftet etwas Subjektives, gar Irrationales an. Es erstaunt daher nicht, dass

in comparison to a rectangular one. While the corners of a space defined by a right angle represent a clear break, obtuse angles underline the integrity of the façade surfaces, i.e., the continuity of the spaces in the interior. This not only strengthens the unity of the building volume but also optimally corresponds to the principle of the one room house: polygonal geometries underscore the "flowing" element of the spatial sequence as the transitions become "smoother" without needing an organic form. For the aforementioned Villa Wehtje ←D Josef Frank combined oblique-angled, orthogonal and organic forms. In 1931 he describes the advantages of polygonal spaces from his point of view: "The right-angled room is the type of room least suited for living in. It is very practical for storing furniture in, but not for anything else. I think that if one were to draw a random polygon with right angles or with obtuse ones, it would be a far more appropriate room layout than any regular right-angled shape. In the top-floor studio apartments, the random irregularities were a great help, and they almost always make for a congenial and somewhat personal atmosphere."[9]

In his later text "Akzidentismus" (1958) [Accidentism] Frank programmatically proclaims chance as a means of design to counter the monotony and sterility of purely functional approaches to form. Thereby he did not intend arbitrariness but a certain measure of freedom: "What we need is a much higher degree of elasticity, not stringent principles of shape[…]."[10] This kind of elasticity, to respond to specific requirements with specific forms, finds its congenial expression in polygonal spaces. At least that is what the oblique geometries suggest. They seem — regardless if they actually are or not — more subjective than rectangular spaces. In our technologized world the orthogonal represents rationality. In contrast, something subjective, even irrational adheres to the polygonal. It is therefore not surprising that Emilio Donato in his analysis of José Antonio Coderch's Ugalde House (1952) ←H, a masterpiece of a geometrically complex spatial sequence, sees the orthogonal principle as being overlaid by a "Dionysian, yet controlled Surrealistic pirouette."[11]

Walter Gropius is also concerned with the opposition between the Apollonian and Dionysian in the foreword to his collection of essays *Apollo in der Demokratie* (1967) [Apollo in the Democracy]: "The eternal pendulum between ways of thinking in art and architecture swings from the Dionysian pole to the Apollonian, from frenzy and chaos to restraint and harmonious moderation.

---

9   Zitiert nach: Bergquist, Mikael und Michélsen, Olof, *Josef Frank Falsterbovillorna*, Stockholm 1998, S. 16.

10   Ursprünglich erschienen in der Zeitschrift *Form*, Nr. 54, 1958. Wieder abgedruckt und zitiert nach: Bergquist, Mikael und Michélsen, Olof (Hg.), *Josef Frank Architektur*, Basel/Boston/Berlin 1995, S. 136.

9   Cited from: Mikael Bergquist and Olof Michélsen, *Accidentism Josef Frank*, translated into English by Ruth Kvarnström (Basel/Boston/Berlin 2005), 13.

10   Originally published in the magazine *Form*, no. 54, 1958. Reprinted in and cited from: Mikael Bergquist and Olof Michélsen, *Accidentism Josef Frank*, translated into English by Ruth Kvarnström (Basel/Boston/Berlin 2005), 20.

11   Emilio Donato, "The Young Coderch," in: Carlos Fochs (ed.), *J.A. Coderch de Sentmenat 1913–1984* (Barcelona 1990), 235.

Typen und Typologien — Orthogonale versus polygonale Räume

Emilio Donato in einer Analyse von José Antonio Coderchs Wohnhaus Ugalde (1952) ←H, einem Meisterwerk eines geometrisch komplexen Raumgefüges, das orthogonale Prinzip von einer «dionysischen, aber kontrollierten, surrealistischen Pirouette» überlagert sieht.[11]

Den Gegensatz des Apollinischen und Dionysischen bemüht auch Walter Gropius im Vorwort seiner Aufsatzsammlung *Apollo in der Demokratie* (1967): «Das ewige Pendel der Geisteshaltung in der Kunst und Architektur schwingt vom dionysischen Pol zum apollinischen, von Rausch und Chaos zu Beherrschung und harmonischem Mass. Selbst im individuellen Künstler befinden sich diese polaren Gegensätze in ständigem Kampf und Ausgleich.»[12] Wie in den Bauten von Coderch, dessen Werk streng orthogonale und solche mit schiefen Winkeln umfasst, so lässt sich auch anhand der Wohnhäuser von Luca Selva Architekten das Vorurteil des Willkürlichen, das der Abweichung vom rechten Winkel tendenziell anhaftet, entkräften: Diese Entwürfe sind nicht weniger bewusst gestaltet und im Modell auf ihre Wirkung hin überprüft, als solche mit traditionell orthogonalen Räumen. Es handelt sich weniger um zwei Pole als verschiedene Dialekte derselben Sprache: Je nach Situation und Anforderung verwenden Luca Selva Architekten orthogonale, polygonale oder Räume beider Gattungen. Ziel ist immer eine Selbstverständlichkeit im Ausdruck und Erleben der Häuser.

Diese Entspanntheit im Umgang mit geometrischen Systemen basiert auf langjähriger Erfahrung, und sie ist eingebettet in die seit Ende der 1990er-Jahre zu beobachtende Tendenz, insbesondere der Deutschschweizer Architektur, hin zu komplexen Formen. Der «Abschied von der Askese»[13], der Übergang von der international viel beachteten «Swiss Box» zu den «Swiss Shapes» – wie 2006 eine Ausstellung in Berlin postulierte –, das heisst die Ersetzung einfacher durch aufwendigere Formen, ist kein singulärer Prozess, sondern ein wiederkehrendes Phänomen der Architekturgeschichte. So hat etwa Robert Venturi in seinem epochemachenden Buch *Komplexität und Widerspruch in der Architektur* (1966) auf das Potenzial schiefwinkliger Elemente hingewiesen, die beispielsweise bei Alvar Aalto und Le Corbusier das reduzierte Vokabular der klassischen Moderne bereichern.[14]

Neben einer Steigerung der Komplexität sind polygonale Formen auch, wie weiter oben beschrieben, ein geeignetes Mittel, einzelne Zimmer zu einem Raumgefüge oder vielgestaltige Gebäudekörper zu einer Einheit zusammenzubinden. Die Verbindung disparater Teile zu einem

Types and Typologies — Orthogonal versus Polygonal Spaces

Even in the individual artist these polar opposites exist in perpetual battle and adjustment."[12] Just as in the buildings of Coderch, whose works include strictly orthogonal as well as oblique angles, the residential buildings by Luca Selva Architects also refute the prejudice of arbitrariness that tends to adhere to deviations from the right angle: these designs are not any less deliberately conceived nor is their effect less carefully assessed in models than those with traditional orthogonal spaces. The matter is less an issue of two opposing poles than different dialects of the same language: depending on the situation and requirements, Luca Selva Architects uses orthogonal, polygonal or spaces of both genres. The aim in the expression and experience of the buildings is always "naturalness."

This nonchalance in dealing with geometrical systems is based on many years of experience and embedded in a general tendency towards complex forms that has been discernable since the late 1990s, especially among Swiss-German architects. The "Abschied von der Askese" [Farewell to Austerity],[13] the transition from the internationally renowned "Swiss Box" to "Swiss Shapes" – as an exhibition in Berlin in 2006 postulated – i.e., the replacement of simple with more complicated forms, is not a singular process but rather a recurring phenomenon in architectural history. In this sense in his epochal book *Complexity and Contradiction in Architecture* (1966) Robert Venturi already pointed to the potential of oblique elements, referring, for instance, to Alvar Aalto's and Le Corbusier's enrichment of the reduced formal vocabulary of Classical Modernism.[14]

In addition to increasing complexity polygonal shapes, as described earlier, are also a suitable means of joining single rooms into a spatial sequence or interlacing multifaceted building volumes into a unit. Connecting disparate parts into a contiguous whole is one of the main features of folded architecture as described by Greg Lynn in *Folding in Architecture* (1993), his programmatic issue of the American magazine *Architectural Design*.[15] This trend has had hardly any direct impact on Swiss architecture, but it possibly encouraged acceptance of shapes deviating from the right angle in the subconscious of architects and their clients. Luca Selva Architects uses the potential of spatial folds mainly in volumetric terms. Beginning with House for Art Collectors ←F and continuing up to House M. ←A, the folds not only create specific building volumes tailored to the plot but also produce contained yet open exterior spaces as part of the garden.

---

11 Donato, Emilio, «The Young Coderch», in: Carlos Fochs (Hg.), *J.A. Coderch de Sentmenat 1913–1984*, Barcelona 1990, S. 235.

12 Gropius, Walter, *Apollo in der Demokratie* (Neue Bauhausbücher), Mainz/Berlin 1967, S. 9.

13 Wieser, Christoph, «Abschied von der Askese», in: Kristin Feireiss/Hans-Jürgen Comerell (Hg.), *Swiss Shapes. Junge Schweizer Architekten*, (Ausst. Kat. Aedes, Berlin) Berlin 2006, S. 2.

14 Venturi, Robert, *Komplexität und Widerspruch in der Architektur* (Bauwelt Fundamente 50), Braunschweig 1978, S. 77.

12 Translation from: Walter Gropius, *Apollo in der Demokratie* (Neue Bauhausbücher), edited by Hans M. Wingler (Mainz/Berlin 1967), 9.

13 Christoph Wieser, "Abschied von der Askese," in: Kristin Feireiss and Hans-Jürgen Comerell (eds.), *Swiss Shapes. Junge Schweizer Architekten,* exhib. cat. (Berlin 2006), 2.

14 Robert Venturi, *Complexity and Contradiction in Architecture* (New York/Chicago 1966), see 72 as well as pp. 18, 19, 41, 44, 50, 52, 82. In German: *Komplexität und Widerspruch in der Architektur* (Bauwelt Fundamente 50) (Braunschweig 1978), in particular 77.

kontinuierlichen Ganzen ist ein Hauptmerkmal gefalteter Architektur, wie sie Greg Lynn in *Folding in Architecture* (1993), seiner programmatischen Nummer der amerikanischen Zeitschrift *Architectural Design*, beschrieben hat.[15] In der Schweizer Architektur fand diese Strömung kaum direkten Niederschlag, beförderte aber möglicherweise im Unterbewussten von Architekten und Bauherrschaften die Akzeptanz für vom rechten Winkel abweichende Formen. Das Potenzial räumlicher Faltungen nutzen Luca Selva Architekten insbesondere in den Volumetrien. Angefangen beim Wohnhaus für Kunstsammler ←F bis hin zum Wohnhaus M. ←A erzeugen die Faltungen sowohl spezifische, auf das Grundstück zugeschnittene Gebäudekörper als auch gefasste und gleichzeitig offene, dem Garten zugehörige Aussenräume.

Ein deutlicher Unterschied zwischen dem geometrischen und dem erlebten Raum, wie ihn Bollnow beschrieben hat, offenbart sich im Vergleich polygonaler und orthogonaler Raumsysteme: Während schiefwinklige Grundrisse auf dem Plan oft geheimnisvoller und komplexer erscheinen als rechtwinklige, muss dem in Wirklichkeit nicht so sein. Bestes Beispiel dafür ist das Wohnhaus beim Wenkenpark. Das im Grundriss einfach anmutende Dispositiv erweist sich an Ort dank verschiedenster diagonaler sowie orthogonaler Sicht- und Raumbezüge als äusserst vielfältig und komplex. Damit ist es repräsentativ für die Arbeit des Basler Büros: Der räumliche Reichtum in Kombination mit einer handwerklich und konstruktiv hochstehenden Materialisierung sowie atmosphärisch stimmiger Ausstrahlung verleiht den Wohnbauten von Luca Selva Architekten eine zeitlose Qualität.

The distinct difference between geometrical/mathematical and experienced space, as Bollnow describes it, is revealed in the comparison of polygonal and orthogonal spatial systems. While oblique ground plans often look more mysterious and complex than rectangular ones, this is not necessarily true in reality. One of the best examples is House at Wenkenpark. The seemingly simple *dispositif* in the ground plan proves in situ to be surprisingly multifaceted and complex thanks to an array of various diagonal and orthogonal visual and spatial relationships. This makes it representative of the work of the Basel firm: spatial richness combined with high-standard materialization in terms of both craftsmanship and constructive solutions as well as atmospherically-coherent presence lend the residential buildings of Luca Selva Architects a timeless quality.

---

15 Lynn, Greg, «Architectural Curvilinearity. The Folded, the Pliant, and the Supple», in: *Folding in Architecture, Architectural Design*, Profile 102, 3/4 1993. Hier verwendet: revised edition 2004, S. 24.

15 Greg Lynn, "Architectural Curvilinearity. The Folded, the Pliant, and the Supple," in: *Folding in Architecture, Architectural Design,* profile 102, 3/4 1993. Used here: revised edition (London 2004), 24.

A

Gartenpavillon
Allschwil, 2005

Garden Pavilion
Allschwil, 2005

Ein Sockel und ein Dach, auf Distanz gehalten durch einen betonierten Kern mit zweiseitig benutzbarem Cheminée sowie vier schlanke Massivholzstützen – das sind die architektonischen Bestandteile des Gartenpavillons. Seine Wirkung ist annähernd so elementar wie die berühmte Skizze eines chinesischen Tempels von Jørn Utzon, die auf Sockel und Dach reduziert ist. Gleichzeitig eignet dem Pavillon eine capricciohafte Leichtigkeit, hervorgerufen durch die polygonale Grundrissform, die das Gebäude im Garten verortet, und durch das Dach, das auf dem Betonkern zu balancieren scheint. Tatsächlich fungieren die Stützen im Wesentlichen als Zugelemente zur Aufnahme der windbedingten Auftriebskräfte; die Konstruktion ist im Gleichgewicht. Gegen Westen ist die exponierte Hälfte des Pavillons mit verschiebbaren, rahmenlosen Glasscheiben schliessbar, die andere Seite ist offen.

Es kommen nur vier verschiedene Materialien zum Einsatz: Lärchenholz, vorpatiniertes Kupfer, Beton und Glas. Dazu ein schmales Kiesbeet zur Aufnahme des vom Dach herunterrinnenden Regenwassers. Über die spezifische Art der Fügung wird die tatsächliche Stärke der Materialien verborgen, es sind nur Oberflächen sichtbar. So wird die körperhafte Wirkung des mit Kupfer verkleideten Sockels und des ebenfalls kupfernen Daches subtil unterwandert, die Materialien verlieren ihr spezifisches Gewicht und erscheinen flächig-abstrakt. Zudem wird die Zusammengehörigkeit von Boden und Deckenuntersicht, die beide in Lärchenholz ausgeführt sind, betont. Dieses von Donald Judd in seinem Atelier an der Spring Street in New York erstmals verwendete Thema haben Luca Selva Architekten bereits 2001 beim Doppelwohnhaus Bäumlihof aufgegriffen. Beim Gartenpavillon ersetzt der starke visuelle Bezug von Boden und Decke die fehlenden Wände, sodass der offene Raum eigentümlich gefasst erscheint.

Mitarbeit: Christoph Rothenhöfer
Holzbau: Louis Risi AG, Allschwil
Fotos: Adriano A. Biondo

A plinth and a roof, kept at a distance by a concrete core with a fireplace usable from both sides and four slim solid-wood pillars — these are the architectonic building blocks of Garden Pavilion, whose effect is nearly as elementary as that of the renowned sketch by Jørn Utzon in which a Chinese temple is reduced to plinth and roof. At the same time the pavilion has a kind of capriccio-like lightness to it, engendered through its polygonal ground plan, which locates the building in the garden, and through the roof, which seems to balance on the concrete core. Actually the pillars essentially serve as tension members to counter the uplift load of the wind force; the construction is balanced. To the west the exposed side of the pavilion can be closed with sliding frameless glass panels, while the other side is open.

Only four different materials have been used: larch, pre-patinated copper, concrete and glass. In addition, a narrow strip of gravel catches rainwater that runs down from the roof. Through the specific way of jointing, the actual force of the materials is hidden: only surfaces are visible. This subtly subverts the voluminous effect of the copper-clad plinth and also clad-incopper roof. The materials thereby lose their specific weight and appear two-dimensionally abstract. In addition, coherence of floor and underside of the roof (i.e., ceiling) is accentuated by executing both elements in larch. First used by Donald Judd in his studio-house on Spring Street in New York, Luca Selva Architects already worked with this theme at Bäumlihof Duplex in 2001. At Garden Pavilion the strong visual connection between floor and ceiling replaces the missing walls so that curiously enough the open space appears contained.

Staff: Christoph Rothenhöfer
Wood Construction: Louis Risi AG, Allschwil
Photos: Adriano A. Biondo

B

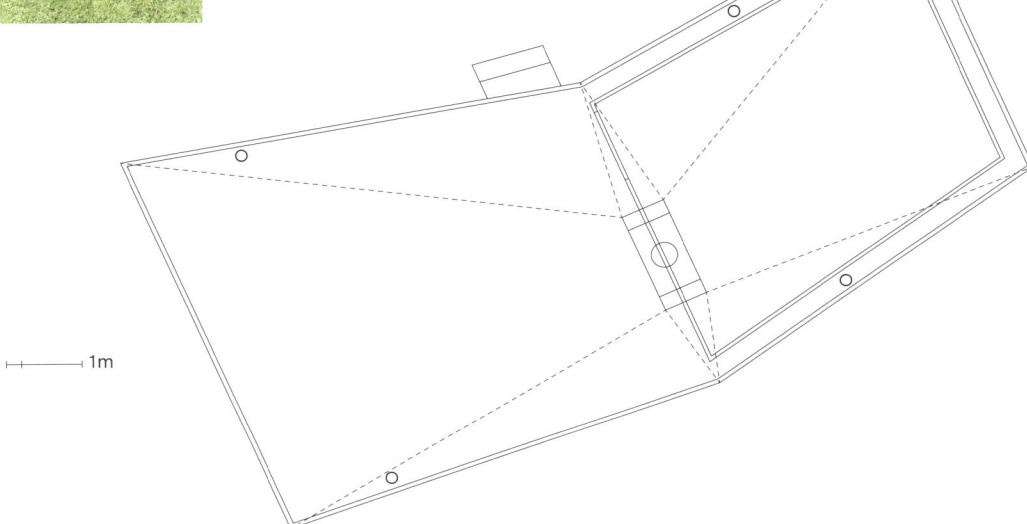

|—| 1m

C

D

E

Luca Selva in Conversation with Daniel Buchner

Moderated by Christoph Wieser

Design Liberty as Chance and Challenge

CW   The first project of an architectural firm is often a single family house. Luca, is that true of your career as well?

LS   No, after winning a competition early on, the first project we built was a schoolhouse. Kaltbrunnen Schoolhouse in Basel (1996) →A was created in cooperation with Jean-Pierre Wymann. Five years later, by then with my own office, we were able to realize the first dwelling — Bäumlihof Duplex (2001) →C in Riehen.

CW   What was it like for you, Daniel?

DB   After an initial failed attempt to establish an office by participating in competitions, some years later we started out by realizing diverse small projects and conversions. It still took a few more years before we built our first "full-fledged" new single family house project, House in Blonay (2002) →F G H.

CW   What significance does the single family house have in your firms today?

DB   That's hard to say. It is certainly a type of architectural commission that has been a constant part of our practice. We appreciate these projects very much and enjoy working on them.

LS   Residential buildings gave our office an identity when we didn't have other commissions. They have helped to make our work publicly known and were important for us in developing an office and execution culture. Personally I find the single family house to be a difficult program. There are always ambitious clients behind it who want to represent themselves through the project. What's expected is haute couture. These highly individualized expectations create a challenging situation from the beginning.

Leeway and Limits

CW   So why do you continue doing single family houses despite all the difficulties and challenges?

DB   It's the intensity of the investigation that I like. The clients are almost always laypersons when it comes to building, not consortia who know exactly what is right and wrong. As a rule they have a great openness. Starting from their wishes

Luca Selva im Gespräch mit Daniel Buchner Spielraum und Grenzen Luca Selva in Conversation with Daniel Buchner Leeway and Limits

sind fast immer Baulaien, keine Konsortien, die genau wissen, was richtig und falsch ist. Sie bringen in der Regel eine grosse Offenheit mit. Ausgehend von ihren Wünschen und Ideen versuchen wir, etwas Einzigartiges oder Spezifisches zu entwickeln.

cw   Ist somit die Übersetzung der persönlichen Wohnvorstellungen der Bauherrschaft in eine architektonische Form gleichzeitig Methode und Faszination bei der Planung eines Einfamilienhauses?

db   Ja, es gilt für den Ort und das Programm die passende Lösung zu finden. Wenn wir beispielsweise Genossenschaftswohnungen bauen, ist die thematische Auseinandersetzung mit der Bauherrschaft oftmals viel kleiner als bei Einfamilienhäusern, wo es eine oder zwei Ansprechpersonen gibt. Der Spielraum beim Entwerfen ist aber auch deshalb grösser, weil das Raumprogramm viel flexibler gestaltet werden kann.

cw   Ist die entwerferische Freiheit bei Einfamilienhäusern effektiv am grössten?

ls   Auf jeden Fall. Es handelt sich um Laborsituationen, bei denen man sich auf etwas Neues einlassen kann, auf Programme, die man so noch nie bearbeitet hat. Es macht Freude, diese speziellen Wohnvorstellungen zu verräumlichen. Gleichzeitig ist dieser Prozess nirgends so komplex wie beim Einfamilienhaus. Es kann deshalb auch passieren, dass man sich nicht findet.

db   Die Kommunikation mit der Bauherrschaft ist in der Tat sehr aufwendig und krisenanfällig, deshalb investieren wir viel Zeit in den Aufbau gegenseitigen Vertrauens. Planung und Bau lösen bei den Auftraggebern starke Emotionen aus. Solche Schwankungen kommen bei grossen Objekten, etwa wenn man für eine Gemeinde baut, viel seltener vor.

ls   Man spürt nirgends so unmittelbar wie beim Einfamilienhaus, dass Bauen existenziell ist – auch wenn man sich natürlich eher in einer «Komfortzone» bewegt. Jeder Entscheid betrifft die eigene Existenz. Deshalb kann man die Aufmerksamkeit gegenüber der Bauherrschaft innerhalb des Büros auch kaum delegieren.

db   Tatsächlich sind Einfamilienhäuser die unrentabelsten Aufgaben, erfordern aber die höchste Präsenz der Büroinhaber. Schön ist jedoch, dass die Bauherrschaft zu 100 Prozent entscheidungsfähig ist. Grössere Konsortien dagegen entscheiden nicht für sich selbst, sondern suchen nach breiter Abstützung, was eine gewisse Trägheit mit sich bringt. Bei Einfamilienhäusern geschieht alles unmittelbar und direkt. Deshalb kann

and ideas, we try to develop something unique or specific.

cw   Does that mean that translating the client's personal concepts of dwelling into an architectural form is both method and fascination in the planning of a single family house?

db   Yes, what's important is to find a suitable solution for the site and program. When we design cooperative apartments, e.g., the thematic investigation with the client is often much less than with single family houses where there are only one or two contact persons. However, the leeway in designing is therefore also much greater because the spatial program can be more flexibly designed.

cw   Are design liberties the greatest with single family houses?

ls   By all means. It's a laboratory situation where something new can be allowed to happen, programs that have never been worked on this way before. It is a pleasure to spatialize these special ideas of dwelling. At the same time this process is never more complex than with the single family house. Therefore it can happen that no common ground is found.

db   The communication with clients is actually quite time consuming and crisis prone, which is why we invest a lot of time into building up mutual trust. Planning and construction usually bring out very strong emotions in clients. Such swings occur much less often with larger projects, e.g., when working with municipalities.

ls   Nowhere else is the existentiality of building more immediate than with the single family house – even if we are operating naturally in somewhat of a "comfort zone." Each decision affects someone's own existence. That's why it is almost impossible to delegate attending to the client to someone else in the office.

db   As a matter of fact single family houses are the most unremunerative commissions while requiring the greatest degree of presence of the firm owner. However, what's nice is that the client is 100 percent able to make his or her own decisions. In contrast, larger consortia don't decide for themselves but search for broader support, which ultimately involves a certain inertia. With single family houses everything happens immediately and directly. Therefore the design process can be steered in a much more focused way by the architect.

cw   Does this also mean that an architect's signature is considerably more readable with a single family house than with other commissions?

A
Kaltbrunnen-Schulhaus, Basel 1996
Kaltbrunnen Schoolhouse, Basel 1996

B
Wohnsiedlung Densa-Areal, Basel 2011
Densa-Areal Residential Complex, Basel 2011

C
Doppelwohnhaus Bäumlihof, Riehen 2001
Bäumlihof Duplex, Riehen 2001

D
Wohnhaus beim Wenkenpark, Riehen 2004
House at Wenkenpark, Riehen 2004

E
Wohnhaus für Künstler, Lupsingen 2005
House for Artists, Lupsingen 2005

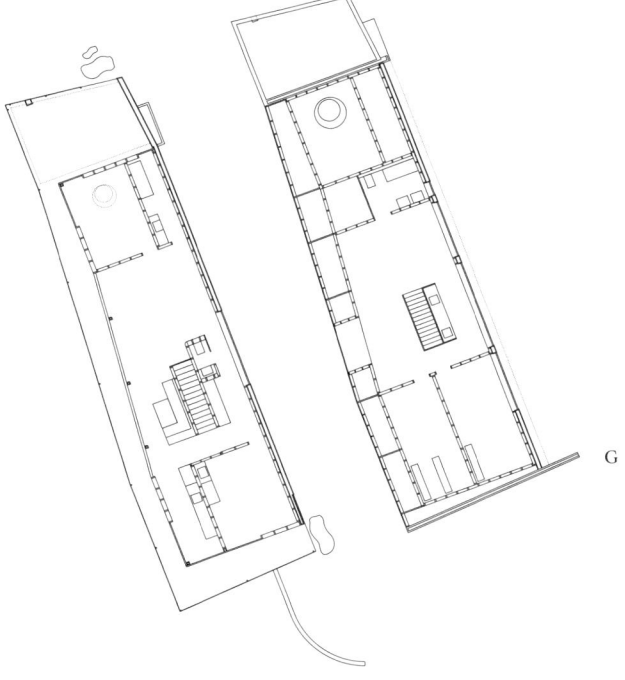

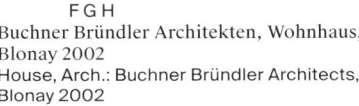

F G H
Buchner Bründler Architekten, Wohnhaus, Blonay 2002
House, Arch.: Buchner Bründler Architects, Blonay 2002

I J K
Buchner Bründler Architekten, Wohnhaus Bläsiring, Basel 2012
House on Bläsiring, Arch.: Buchner Bründler Architects, Basel 2012

Luca Selva im Gespräch mit Daniel Buchner — Einfamilienhaus als Entwurfslabor

der Entwurfsprozess vom Architekten viel gezielter gesteuert werden.

CW   Ist somit auch die Handschrift der Architekten bei einem Einfamilienhaus deutlicher lesbar als bei anderen Aufgaben?

DB   Oft habe ich das Gefühl, je kleiner die Bauaufgabe, desto intensiver die Auseinandersetzung. Wenn du einen einzigen Raum planst, beschäftigst du dich mit allen vier Wänden, bei 200 geht das nicht mehr. Grosse Aufgaben lassen es kaum zu, jeden Winkel zu studieren – was letztlich Bauen ausmacht. Bei Grossprojekten sind die Rahmenbedingungen oft so vereinnehmend, dass man den Bezug zur eigentlichen Aufgabe teilweise zu verlieren droht.

LS   Man könnte sagen, das Einfamilienhaus sei die kanonische Form der Architektur, weil man mit allen Fragen direkt in Berührung kommt: Man kann alle Entscheide selber herbeiführen, alles selber zeichnen, mit den Gummistiefeln auf der Baustelle stehen und wenn nötig selbst Hand anlegen. Das Errichten eines Wohnhauses hat etwas Archetypisches.

Einfamilienhaus als Entwurfslabor

CW   Ihr habt vom Einfamilienhaus als Entwurfslabor gesprochen. Gibt es konkrete Dinge, die ihr ausprobiert und anschliessend übertragen habt?

LS   Wir hätten uns beispielsweise kaum getraut, die Wohnsiedlung Densa-Areal (2011) ←B in Klinker auszuführen, wenn wir vorher nicht bereits das Wohnhaus beim Wenkenpark (2004) ←D in Klinker gebaut hätten. So konnten wir grundlegende Dinge durchspielen: Wie bildet man in Klinker eine Ecke aus, wie wird abgedichtet, wie werden hohe Wände erstellt? Das gab uns die Zuversicht, mit diesem Material gut zu arbeiten. Im Lauf der Jahre entsteht ein Know-how, das nicht nur in anderen Situationen schnell abrufbar ist, sondern auch als Referenzbeispiel für Bauherrschaften herangezogen werden kann. Ähnliches gilt auf typologischer Ebene, wobei diese Lösungen schwieriger zu übertragen sind, da eine Wohnsiedlung grundsätzlich anders funktioniert als ein Einfamilienhaus.

DB   In erster Linie suchen wir für jedes Projekt nach einer grundlegenden Idee. Die Erfahrungen fliessen natürlich in die folgenden Häuser ein. Detaillierungen etwa, die in ähnlicher Form aufgegriffen werden. Auch typologische Erfahrungen können übertragen werden, sei es der Umgang mit offenen Räumen, mit der Proportionierung, der Ausbildung von Wegverbindungen. Es gibt immer

DB   I often have the feeling that the smaller a project, the more intense the investigation. When you plan a single room you pay attention to all four walls; with 200, that is no longer possible. Large commissions hardly allow for studying every angle or corner – which eventually is what building is all about. With large projects the framework conditions are often so engrossing that there's a risk of losing the connection to the actual tasks.

LS   One could say that the single family house is the canonical form of architecture because one comes into direct contact with all the questions: you can make all the decisions yourself, draw everything yourself, stand on the building site in rubber boots and, if necessary, even lend a hand in the construction. Erecting a dwelling has something archetypical.

Single Family House as Design Laboratory

CW   You spoke earlier about the single family house as design laboratory. Are there concrete things that you have tried out and subsequently transferred?

LS   We would hardly have dared, e.g., to execute Densa-Areal Residential Complex (2011) ←B in clinker if we hadn't already built House at Wenkenpark (2004) ←D in the same material. This made it possible to explore fundamental things: How do you shape a corner in clinker? How do you use the sealant? How are high walls constructed? That experience gave us the confidence to work well with this material. Over the years know-how accumulates, which, on the one hand, is not only quickly accessible in other situations but can also be drawn upon as a referential example for clients. The same is true on a typological level, although these solutions are much harder to transfer, because a residential complex functions in a completely different way than a single family house.

DB   First of all for every project we search for a fundamental idea. Experience naturally flows into subsequent houses. Detailing, e.g., is taken up again in a similar form. Typological experience can also be transferred, be it in the treatment of open space, proportioning or developing circulation connections. There will always be solutions, that I feel are successful and that I want to draw upon again later.

CW   Are you thinking of something concrete?

DB   In the case of detailing, e.g., the treatment of doors. For us, material and haptic qualities are decisive. For our houses we often use

wieder Lösungen, die ich als geglückt empfinde und auf die ich später wieder zurückgreifen möchte.

CW Denkst du an etwas Konkretes?

DB Im Fall von Detaillierungen zum Beispiel an den Umgang mit Türen. Material und Haptik sind für uns entscheidend. Oft verwenden wir bei unseren Häusern Zapfenbandtüren mit tiefen Griffleisten, die wir immer wieder weiterentwickeln. Teilweise erproben wir auch Gegenpositionen zu unserer bisherigen Arbeit. Ging es beim Lofthaus in Basel (2002) etwa um einen offenen Grundriss mit grossen Öffnungen, experimentieren wir derzeit mit räumlicher und atmosphärischer Dichte und der damit verbundenen Frage, wie viel Tageslicht wirklich nötig ist. Bei uns entstehen die Häuser oft vom Kern aus, die Fassaden denken wir konzeptuell mit, formalisieren sie aber meist spät – was bei Wettbewerben teilweise ein Problem ist.

CW Habt ihr ebenfalls ein gängiges Entwurfsverfahren?

LS Wir gehen üblicherweise vom Raum aus, von der Art, wie der Grundriss eingeteilt ist – offen oder gekammert – und wie die Räume sich gegen aussen öffnen. Wir bauen früh 1:20-Modelle, um die Raumwirkung und Lichtstimmung zu entwickeln, noch bevor wir uns Gedanken zur Materialisierung machen. Wie die Fenster in der Wand sitzen, wo und in welcher Grösse, ob sie frontal oder lateral wahrgenommen werden beschäftigt uns sehr.

CW Ihr habt gesagt, die Einfamilienhäuser seien vom ökonomischen Standpunkt aus für das Büro eher eine Belastung. Bei grossen Projekten dagegen ist mehr Luft für Entwicklungen vorhanden.

DB Das stimmt, was typologische, räumliche und situationsbezogene Fragen angeht. Allerdings werden grosse Projekte oft in kurzer Zeit realisiert, kleine dagegen ziehen sich in die Länge und bieten Zeit für Entwicklungen. Bei Grossprojekten sind die Prozesse viel stringenter und strukturierter. Zudem ist man oft von General- und Totalunternehmen abhängig, die nicht sehr experimentierfreudig sind. Bei Einfamilienhäusern hingegen trägst du als Architekt die gesamte Verantwortung, entsprechend grösser ist der Spielraum bei der Realisierung.

LS Grosse Projekte sind auch deutlich weniger lang «modellierfähig». Das heisst, die Entscheidungen fallen viel früher als bei Einfamilienhäusern und können nur mit grossem Aufwand verändert oder gar rückgängig gemacht werden, weil die Entscheidungsabläufe so komplex sind. Bei Einfamilienhäusern hingegen ist es immer wieder

pivot hinge doors with deep grip strips, which we are always redeveloping further. To some extent we also try out the position exactly opposite our previous work. While in Loft House (2002) in Basel, e.g., the concern was an open ground plan with large openings, we are currently experimenting with spatial and atmospheric density and the resulting question of how much daylight is really necessary. With us the houses are created from the core out, along with a conceptual development of the façades, which are, however, usually formalized later – which in competitions can be somewhat of a problem.

CW Do you also have an established design process?

LS We usually start with the space, with the way the ground plan is articulated – open or chambered – and how the spaces are going to open to the outside. Very early on we build 1:20 models to develop the spatial effect and mood of the lighting, even before we start thinking about the materialization. We are very much concerned with how the windows will sit in the wall, where and in what size, if they will be perceived frontally or laterally.

CW You mentioned earlier that from an economical point of view, single family houses are rather a liability. On the other hand, with larger projects there is more leeway for developments.

DB That's true in terms of typological, spatial and situational questions. However, large-scale projects are often realized in a short time, while smaller ones drag on, which offers time for developments. With large projects processes are much more stringent and structured. In addition, one is often dependent on general contractors who are not particularly keen to experiment. In contrast, with single family houses you, as the architect, carry the full responsibility and the leeway in the realization is accordingly greater.

LS The time during which large projects are still "malleable" is also much shorter, i.e., decisions are made much earlier than with single family houses and can only be changed or even reversed with great expenditure, because the decision-making processes are so complex. With single family houses, on the other hand, you always have the possibility to reassess decisions in order to find new, better solutions.

DB The situation of competitions is symptomatic: After three months of intense work what's created along with a fully conceptualized project are some images to show what the project is going to look like. If you win, the clients expect

the building to be realized exactly as it appears in the rendering. It's nearly impossible to get away from this early pre-set image regardless of how massive the program changes. For single family houses we don't work with images, rarely with façades but rather with concepts.

Single Family House as Dwelling Form

CW Luca, you have criticized the single family house as a dwelling form. To what extent do your own ideas of dwelling play a role in the design process?

LS The detached house has never been a topic for me personally; also I've never encountered it in terms of my biography. At least in areas close to cities it is an obsolete model, encourages urban sprawl and inhibits much-needed densification. In less urban areas or in Alpine regions, however, it has been playing an important role for generations as a building form for securing livelihood. This purpose will live on.

DB I spent the first 18 years of my life in a bad single family house, which, however, did not leave a negative impression on me. My parents planned it themselves, which is why I understand the meaning it still has for them today as owners. With every single family house I design, I imagine myself living in it. Only after it is finished do I realize that it does not represent my own ideas but those of the clients — which is good. I live in a two-party townhouse in Basel (2012) ←IJK that was designed by us, work at an office away from home, additionally rent two garages and a studio for my musical passion and have a study in the countryside. So sometimes I long to bring everything together in one location, e.g., like Peter Zumthor in Haldenstein. From my point of view the single family house can work as a form of dwelling. Unfortunately the leeway is increasingly limited by regulations, but still it's sometimes possible to profit from this situation: we are currently building a single family house in Lörrach →LM. Although the utilization factor is prescribed by the municipality, there is no regulation concerning the building density ratio. Because the walls don't touch the ground, the building does not count as a house, which makes it possible for us to build a huge, barn-like hull.

LS With the single family house the expectation to meet all needs with just this one house is greater than usual. The idea of wanting to explain the whole world with one house is completely foreign to me. On the other hand, there are single family houses that are *Gesamtkunstwerke*.

Luca Selva im Gespräch mit Daniel Buchner — Haus und Garten

Luca Selva in Conversation with Daniel Buchner — House and Garden

Gebäude nicht als Haus, sodass wir eine riesige, scheunenartige Hülle bauen können.

LS Beim Einfamilienhaus ist der Anspruch grösser als sonst, mit diesem einen Haus sämtliche Bedürfnisse abzudecken. Mir ist die Vorstellung fremd, mit einem Haus die ganze Welt erklären zu wollen. Andererseits gibt es Einfamilienhäuser, die Gesamtkunstwerke sind. Palladios Villa Rotonda (1591) ist ein solcher Tempel der Schönheit. Diese Dichte ist fast nur im Einfamilienhaus denkbar, weil die entwerferische Freiheit am grössten ist. Vermutlich gibt es deshalb so viele architekturgeschichtlich bedeutsame Einfamilienhäuser.

Haus und Garten

CW Selten geglückt ist bei der Villa Rotonda auch das Zusammenspiel von Haus und Landschaft. Wie stellt sich bei euren Wohnhäusern das Verhältnis zum Umfeld dar, das heute selbstverständlich viel stärker determiniert ist als damals bei Palladio?

DB Man muss sich mit den Orten auseinandersetzen. Wichtiger jedoch als das konkrete Haus gegenüber ist für uns die Art der Bebauung, die Höhen, die Körnung des Quartiers, die Präsenz der Gärten. Aufgrund der kleineren Parzellengrösse ist kaum noch Platz für einen Baum vorhanden, der laut Gesetz einen bestimmten Durchmesser beanspruchen darf. Bäume sind teilweise auch nicht mehr geduldet, weil der Nachbar beispielsweise auf Birken allergisch ist.

LS Der Spielraum für die Setzung und Ausbildung des Volumens ist oft klein, man bewegt sich an der Grenze des Zulässigen. Zudem kristallisieren sich die spezifischen Themen eines Ortes jeweils schnell heraus. In Lupsingen beispielsweise, wo wir ein Wohnhaus für Künstler (2005) ←E gebaut haben, gibt es eine spezielle Schrägdachverordnung und ein Nachbarhaus mit Eternitschindeln. Solche Themen haben wir aufgenommen, verfremdet und damit den Kontext in einen neuen Zusammenhang gestellt. Ein neues Haus ist immer ein Kommentar zum Bestand. Wichtiger ist uns jedoch, die Bedürfnisse der Bauherrschaft mit den Möglichkeiten des Ortes zu verweben. Das bezieht sich auf das Haus und den Garten, der – insbesondere der Aussensitzplatz – oft Hauptgrund für ein Einfamilienhaus ist. Die Beziehung von Haus und Garten ist essenziell und könnte in unserer Arbeit noch vertieft werden.

DB Häufig ist es viel schwieriger, die Bauherrschaft für ein Landschaftkonzept zu

Palladio's Villa Rotonda (1591) is such a temple of beauty. This density is almost only conceivable in the single family house, because the design liberties are the greatest. That's probably why there are so many single family houses of significance in architecture history.

House and Garden

CW A rare feat is also the interplay of house and landscape at Villa Rotonda. With your residential buildings how do you conceive of the relationship to the surroundings, which nowadays is obviously much more determined than at the time of Palladio?

DB The sites have to be thoroughly investigated. But what is more important to us than the specific house vis-à-vis is the type of urban fabric, heights, texture of the neighborhood, presence of gardens. Because of the smaller sizes of the plots, there is hardly space available for a tree, which according to regulations requires a prescribed diameter. Trees are also often no longer tolerated because the neighbor, e.g., is allergic to birch.

LS The leeway in positioning and articulating the volume is often small, one pushes at the limits of what is permitted. Furthermore the specific themes of a place always crystallize quickly. In Lupsingen, e.g., where we built House for Artists (2005) ←E, there is a special pitched roof regulation and a neighboring house with Eternit shingles. We assimilated such themes, defamiliarized them and thereby established a new nexus for the context. A new building is always a comment on the existing built environment. More important for us, however, is to intertwine the needs of the clients with the possibilities of the location. That includes both house and garden, which — especially the seating area outdoors — is often one of the main reasons for building a single family house. The relationship between house and garden is essential and could be further deepened in our work.

DB It's often much more difficult to convince the client to agree to a landscape concept than to a spatial-architectonic one. Maybe that's because they usually have an idea of how a garden should be. With our first houses we somewhat neglected the planning of the surroundings. Today the landscape is already conceived along with the concept for the house.

CW Are there projects in which you begin with the garden?

DB No, but house and garden are considered as a unity. Is there a tree? Where does it

L

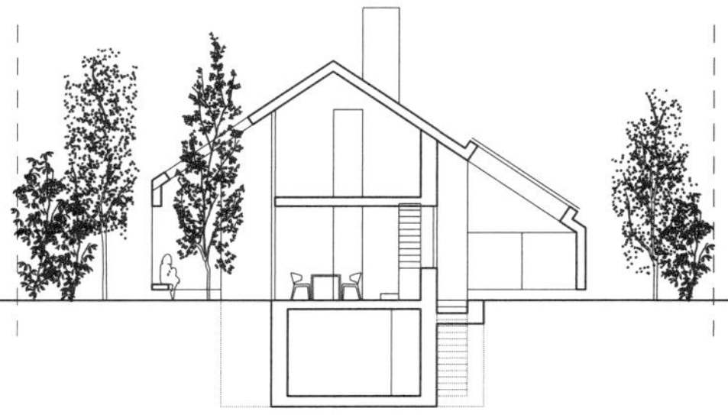

M

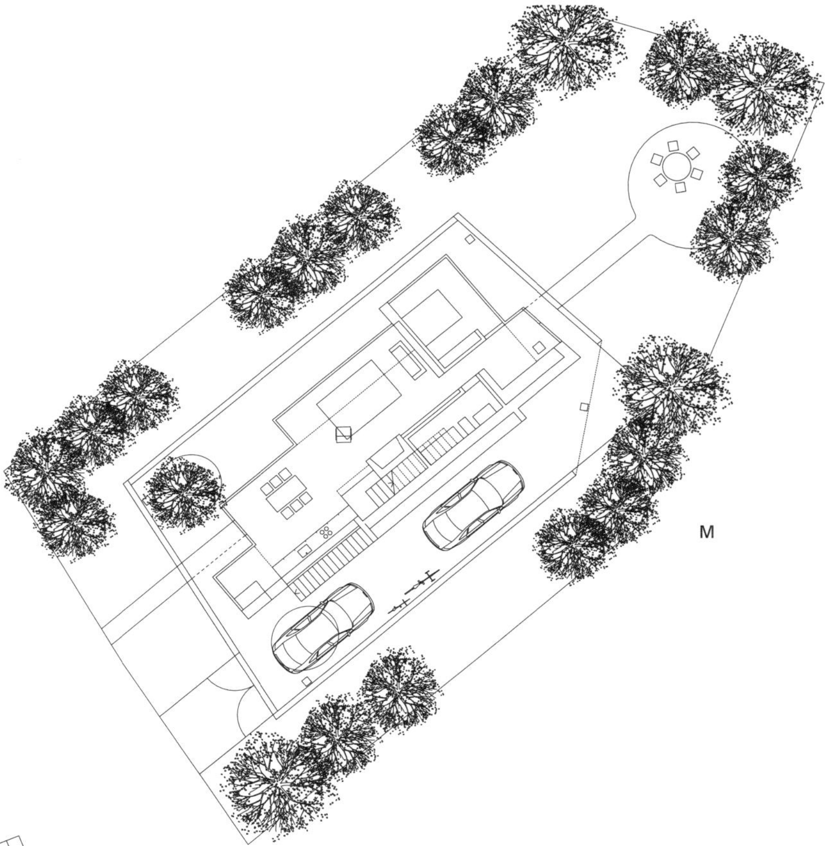

N

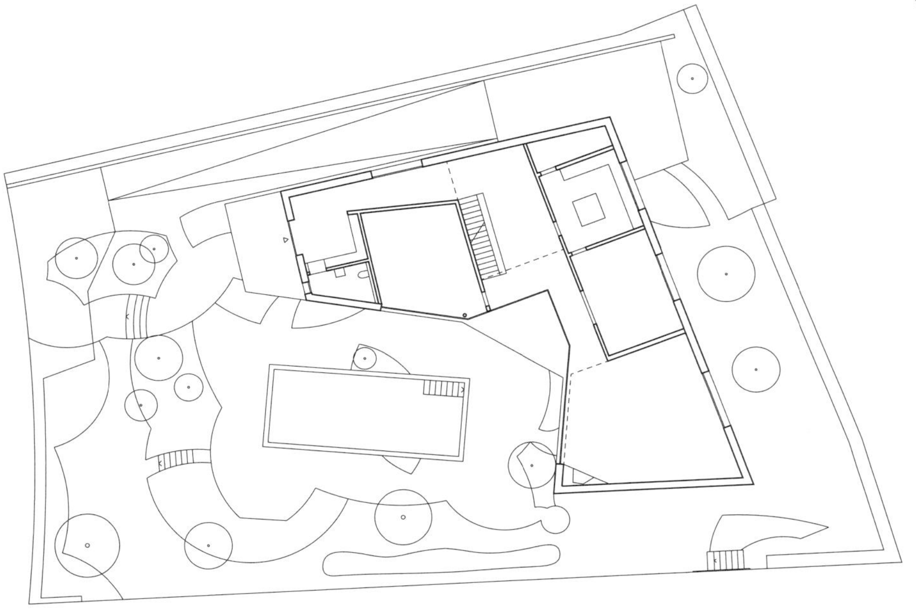

5 m

L M
Buchner Bründler Architekten, Wohnhaus, Lörrach 2014
House, Arch.: Buchner Bründler Architects, Lörrach 2014

N
Wohnhaus für Kunstsammler, Binningen 2008, Umgebungsplan von August + Margrith Künzel Landschaftsarchitekten
House for Art Collectors, Binningen 2008, Situation Plan by August + Margrith Künzel Landschaftsarchitekten

O
Schulhaus Erlenmatt, Basel 2017
Erlenmatt Schoolhouse, Basel 2017

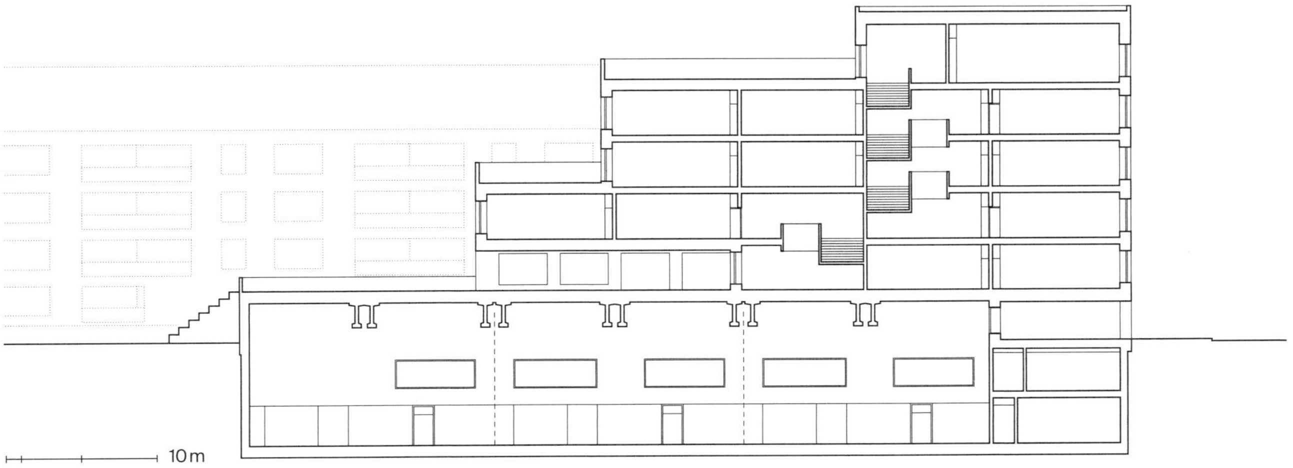

O

10 m

gewinnen, als für ein räumlich-architektonisches. Das hat vielleicht damit zu tun, dass sie eher eine Vorstellung davon haben, wie der Garten sein soll. Wir haben bei unseren ersten Häusern die Planung der Umgebung etwas vernachlässigt. Heute ist beim Konzept für das Haus die Landschaft schon mitgedacht.

CW   Gibt es Projekte, bei denen ihr vom Garten ausgeht?

DB   Nein, aber Haus und Garten sind als Einheit gedacht. Gibt es einen Baum? Wo steht er? Soll es Rasen, Wiese oder Asphalt sein? Geht man ebenerdig oder über Stufen ins Haus? Und so weiter.

LS   Wir machen uns ähnliche Überlegungen. Teils hatten wir es mit sehr grossen Grundstücken zu tun, insbesondere beim Generationenhaus (2013) «21. Hier ging es vor allem darum, das neue Wohnhaus in Einklang zum bestehenden Park zu entwerfen, denn das alte Haus stand zu tief und hatte keinen echten Bezug zum Garten. Bei diesem Projekt arbeiteten wir mit den Landschaftsarchitekten Appert Zwahlen zusammen, beim Wohnhaus für Kunstsammler (2008) ←N mit August und Margrith Künzel.

Dichte und Einfachheit

CW   Ihr habt mit euren Büros zahlreiche Wohnhäuser gebaut. Gibt es Themen, die ihr noch ausloten möchtet, die ihr vielleicht schon einmal ins Auge gefasst habt, aber nicht realisieren konntet?

DB   Unsere Einfamilienhäuser werden im Moment eher dichter und dunkler. Viel Licht ist immer toll; es gibt aber auch sehr schöne etwas dunklere, lichtgeschonte Räume. Das Haus am Bläsiring ist schmal und tief ←IJK. Am liebsten sind mir die Zonen in der Tiefe des Grundrisses, wo nie direktes Sonnenlicht hinkommt. Das Wohnhaus in Lörrach hat etwas höhlenartiges. Wie in alten Bauernhäusern gelangt nur wenig Sonne zu bestimmten Zeiten an ausgesuchten Stellen ins Innere. Das sind solche Raumstimmungen, die wir gerade erforschen.

LS   Mich interessiert, kleinere Häuser ohne übergrosse Räume zu bauen. Bezüglich der Flächen haben wir jedes Mass verloren. Ich staune immer wieder, wie knapp und präzise die Räume in Le Corbusiers Maison La Roche-Jeanneret (1923) sind. Über eine gewisse Verkleinerung können Räume an Reichtum und Aussage gewinnen, was eine elementarere Raumwahrnehmung ermöglicht. Deshalb faszinieren mich die Kleinhäuser in

stand? Should it be a lawn, meadow or asphalt? Does one enter the house from the ground level or via steps? And so on.

LS   We consider similar issues. In some cases we were dealing with very large plots, especially for Generational House (2013) «21. Here our main concern was to put the new residential building in tune with the existing park, because the old house had been placed too deep and didn't really have a proper connection to the garden. We collaborated with the landscape architects Appert Zwahlen on this project and with August and Margrith Künzel on House for Art Collectors (2008) ←N.

Density and Simplicity

CW   With your offices you both have built numerous residential buildings. Are there themes that you would still like to explore, which you maybe already had in mind but couldn't realize?

DB   At the moment our single family houses are becoming denser and darker. It's always great to have a lot of light, but there are also slightly darker rooms, light-protected spaces that are very beautiful. House on Bläsiring (2012) is narrow and deep ←IJK. What I like best are the zones deep inside the ground plan where there is never any direct sunlight. The house in Lörrach is somewhat cave-like. As in old farmhouses, only at certain times of the day does the sun reach select spots in the interior. These are the kinds of spatial moods we are exploring at the moment.

LS   I am interested in building smaller houses without oversized spaces. In terms of surface area we have lost any sense of scale. It never ceases to amaze me how reduced and precise the spaces are in Le Corbusier's Maison La Roche-Jeanneret (1923). Through a certain reduction spaces can gain in richness and statement, which enables an elementary perception of space. That is why I am so fascinated by the small houses in Japan. It is much more difficult to achieve a high degree of complexity with little space. In addition, I am interested in once more simplifying the house constructively to get rid of some of the conventional layers used today. Especially with single family houses one could work much more directly again concerning the materialization, e.g., without floating floors.

DB   You are right, it is a major loss when nowadays even in the single family house every interior door should be 80 cm and every corridor 1.2 m wide. It can be very pleasurable to walk through a room whose walls I can almost physically

Luca Selva im Gespräch mit Daniel Buchner — Dichte und Einfachheit

Japan. Es ist viel schwieriger, eine hohe Komplexität mit wenig Raum zu erreichen. Zudem interessiere ich mich dafür, das Haus in konstruktiver Hinsicht wieder zu vereinfachen, auf einige der heute gängigen Schichten zu verzichten. Gerade bei Einfamilienhäusern könnte man bezüglich Materialisierung wieder viel direkter arbeiten, ohne schwimmende Böden beispielsweise.

DB Du hast Recht. Es ist ein riesiger Verlust, wenn heute sogar im Einfamilienhaus jede Zimmertür 80 Zentimeter und jeder Korridor 1,2 Meter breit sein soll. Es kann sehr angenehm sein, durch einen Raum zu gehen, dessen Wände ich nahezu physisch spüre. Räumliche Dichte hat etwas Schützendes; sie sollte nicht beengend wirken, eher etwas Leichtes, Selbstverständliches ausstrahlen.

LS Diese Selbstverständlichkeit gilt es zu erreichen, auch in der Materialisierung. Deshalb haben wir beim Wohnhaus mit Atelier (2012) »69 und dem Generationenhaus «21 grosse Steinplatten direkt in Sand verlegt. Das hat etwas Unmittelbares, Handwerkliches. Etwas, das ich vom Haus meiner Grossmutter im Tessin kenne: Der Küchenboden war mit Onsernone-Granit belegt. Die Platten waren uneben, deshalb hatten die Stühle drei Beine. Man wusste gar nicht, ob man drinnen oder draussen ist. Solche Erfahrungen prägen. Das Thema der Böden stellt sich in unseren Bauten immer sehr früh als Frage. Für das Wohnhaus beim Wenkenpark «15 etwa wollten die Bauherren von Anfang an einen schönen, massiven Eichenboden. Deshalb haben wir kein Parkett, sondern lange Dielen verlegt. Jedes Mal, wenn ich dort bin, habe ich Freude daran, dass der Boden schwingt und etwas knarrt. Einen «lebendigen» Holzboden planen wir auch beim Schulhaus Erlenmatt (2017) ←o. Wir möchten richtige «Schulstuben» gestalten, da die Kinder die Zimmer ohnehin nur in Hausschuhen betreten. Somit können wir einen einfachen Holzboden verlegen und dank Radiatoren auf den Unterlagsboden verzichten. Diese direkte Art des Bauens gefällt mir. Sie vermittelt etwas von der grundlegenden, existenziellen Erfahrung, die zum Wohnen gehört. Deshalb ist die Beschäftigung mit dem Einfamilienhaus so faszinierend.

sense. Spatial density has something sheltering, it shouldn't feel constrictive but rather exude something light, matter-of-fact.

LS This matter-of-factness also needs to be achieved in terms of the materialization. To this end at House with Studio (2012) »69 and Generational House «21 we had large stone slabs lain directly in sand. This provides something immediate, craftsmanship-like. Something that I know from my grandmother's home in the Ticino: the kitchen floor was laid with natural Onsernone granite. The slabs were uneven, so the chairs had three legs. You didn't know if you were inside or outside. Such experiences leave a lasting impression. The question of flooring as a theme always emerges very early with our buildings. With House at Wenkenpark «15, e.g., the clients knew from the start that they wanted a beautiful solid oak floor. So we didn't use parquet but rather long boards. Every time I'm there I really enjoy the way the floor sways and somewhat creaks. We're also planning a "lively" wood floor for Erlenmatt Schoolhouse (2017) ←o. We would like to create full-fledged *Schulstuben* [traditional classrooms], where children only enter wearing house slippers anyway. So we can install a very simple wooden floor, and using radiators we can completely dispense with the floor underlayment. This direct kind of construction appeals to me. It communicates a sense of the basic, existential experience that is connected to dwelling. That's why dealing with the single family house is so fascinating.

Biografien

Biographies

Luca Selva

Geboren 1962, zunächst Studium der Germanistik, Philosophie und Geschichte an der Universität Basel, dann Architekturstudium an der ETH Zürich, Diplom und Assistenz am ETH-Lehrstuhl von Dolf Schnebli. 1991 Gründung des eigenen Architekturbüros in Basel, seit 1997 Mitglied im BSA und seit 1999 Professor am Institut Architektur der Hochschule für Architektur, Bau und Geomatik der FHNW, Muttenz.

David Gschwind

Geboren 1975, Lehre als Hochbauzeichner, Architekturstudium an der FHBB, Muttenz, und Diplom bei Prof. Annette Spiro. Seit 2004 Mitarbeit bei Luca Selva Architekten und seit 2009 Partner und Mitglied der Geschäftsleitung von Luca Selva Architekten ETH BSA SIA, Basel.

Roger Braccini

Geboren 1978, Schule für Gestaltung Basel, Lehre als Hochbauzeichner, Architekturstudium an der FHBB, Muttenz, Diplom bei Prof. Annette Spiro. 2004–2007 Mitarbeit u. a. bei Diener & Diener Architekten in Basel, seit 2007 bei Luca Selva Architekten. Seit 2012 Partner und Mitglied der Geschäftsleitung von Luca Selva Architekten ETH BSA SIA, Basel.

Christoph Wieser

Geboren 1967, Architekturstudium und Assistenz an der ETH Zürich, Promotion an der ETH Lausanne. 2003–2009 Redaktor der Zeitschrift *werk, bauen + wohnen*, 2009–2013 Leiter Zentrum / Institut Konstruktives Entwerfen am Departement Architektur, Gestaltung und Bauingenieurwesen der ZHAW in Winterthur. Architekturtheoretiker, Publizist, Forscher und Dozent an schweizerischen Fachhochschulen. Lebt und arbeitet in Zürich.

Daniel Buchner

Geboren 1967, Lehre als Hochbauzeichner, dann Architekturstudium an der Ingenieurschule beider Basel. 1994–1997 Mitarbeit bei Morger & Degelo Architekten in Basel. 1997 Gründung von Buchner Bründler Architekten, Basel, zusammen mit Andreas Bründler. 2008–2009 Gastprofessur an der ETH Lausanne, 2010–2012 Gastdozentur an der ETH Zürich. Mitglied im BSA seit 2003.

Helmuth Pauli

Geboren 1949, Lehre als Eisenbetonzeichner und Studium am Abendtechnikum in Zürich als Bauingenieur. 1976–1989 Anstellungen bei Caprez + Noger, St. Gallen, Galser + Saxer AG, Muttenz, und Hans Schaub Ingenieurbüro, Basel. 1989–2001 eigenes Ingenieurbüro für Hoch- und Industriebauten in Basel, 2001–2014 Partner und Vizepräsident des Verwaltungsrates der ZPF Ingenieure AG, Basel. Seit März 2014 pensioniert und beratender Ingenieur.

Martin Rauch

Geboren 1958, Landesfachschule für Keramik und Ofenbau Stoob und Studium in der Meisterklasse für Keramik bei Prof. Maria Bilger-Perz und Prof. Matteo Thun an der Hochschule für angewandte Kunst, Wien. Seit 1990 Konzeption, Planung und Realisierung von Lehmbauprojekten, 1999 Firmengründung Lehm Ton Erde, Baukunst GmbH. Seit 2010 Honorarprofessor des UNESCO-Lehrstuhls «Earthen Architecture», zahlreiche Preise und Auszeichnungen.

Luca Selva

Born 1962, studied German, Philosophy and History at the University of Basel before completing a degree in Architecture at ETH Zurich, where he was assistant to ETH Chair Dolf Schnebli. In 1991 he founded his own architectural firm in Basel. He has been a member of BSA (Association of Swiss Architects) since 1997. Since 1999 he has been professor at the Institute of Architecture, School of Architecture, Civil Engineering and Geomatics, University of Applied Sciences and Arts Northwestern Switzerland (FHNW) in Muttenz.

David Gschwind

Born 1975, educational and training program as building construction draftsperson and studied Architecture at FHBB in Muttenz and finished his diploma under Prof. Annette Spiro. Since 2004 he has been working at Luca Selva Architects ETH BSA SIA, Basel, and since 2009 he has been partner and managing board member there.

Roger Braccini

Born 1978, Basel School of Design, educational and training program as building construction draftsperson and studied architecture at FHBB in Muttenz and finished his diploma under Prof. Annette Spiro. 2004–2007 he worked at, among others, Diener & Diener Architects in Basel. Since 2007 he has been working at Luca Selva Architects ETH BSA SIA, Basel, and since 2012 he has been partner and managing board member there.

Christoph Wieser

Born 1967, studied architecture and worked as an assistant at ETH Zurich. He completed his doctorate at ETH Lausanne. 2003–2009 he worked as an editor for the magazine *werk, bauen + wohnen*. 2009–2013 he was Head at Center/Institute of Constructional Design, Department of Architecture, Design and Civil Engineering, Zurich University of Applied Sciences (ZHAW) in Winterthur. He is an architecture theoretician, publicist, researcher and lecturer at different applied arts and sciences universities in Switzerland. He lives and works in Zurich.

Daniel Buchner

Born 1967, completed an educational and training program as building construction draftsperson before studying architecture at School for Engineering, FHBB in Muttenz. 1994–1997 he worked for Morger & Degelo Architects in Basel and in 1997 founded Buchner Bründler Architects, Basel, together with Andreas Bründler. 2008–2009 he was guest professor at ETH Lausanne; and 2010–2012, visiting lecturer at ETH Zurich. He has been a member of BSA since 2003.

Helmuth Pauli

Born 1949, educational and training program as reinforced concrete draftsperson and studied civil engineering at University of Applied Technologies (HSZ-T, formerly "Abend-Technikum") in Zurich. 1976–1989 he worked at Caprez + Noger, St. Gallen; Galser+Saxer AG, Muttenz; and Hans Schaub Engineers, Basel. 1989–2001, principal of his own engineering firm for civil and industrial construction in Basel; 2001–2014, partner and vice president of the administrative board at ZPF Ingenieure AG, Basel. In March 2014 he retired and since then has been working as an engineering consultant.

Martin Rauch

Born 1958, attended Technical College of Ceramics and Oven Construction, Stoob, and master class in ceramics under Prof. Maria Bilger-Perz and Prof. Matteo Thun at University of Applied Arts, Vienna. Since 1990 he has been designing, planning and realizing loam building projects and in 1999 founded his own firm Lehm Ton Erde, Baukunst GmbH. Since 2010, he has been an honorary professor at the UNESCO Chair of Earthen Architecture and has won numerous prizes and awards.

Mitarbeitende seit 1993
Current Staff Members
since 1993

Luca Selva
David Gschwind
Roger Braccini
Alex Pipoz
Sigrid Vierzigmann
Gian Andrea Serena
Jonathan Benhamu
Sonja Christen
Olivia Frei
Claudia Agné
Véronique Caviezel
Raphaël Oehler
Petra Waldburger
Sabine Bruinink
Laia Solé
Lukas Schirmann
Vanessa Kuc
Armin Schärer
Marie-Annick Horton
Daniela Bader
Sonja Keller
Céline Reber
Federica Garabelli
Irene Giubbini
Annabelle Gawaz
Yannick Perroud

(Reihenfolge gemäss Eintritt)
(in chronological order based
on earliest starting date)

Ehemalige Mitarbeitende
Former Staff Members

Roman Albertini
Barbara Andres
Alexandra Bair
Kora Balmer
Lukas Baumann
Anouk Benon
Julia Borbely
Frederic Borruat
Michèle Brand
Gabriel Brodmann
Melanie Camenzind
Giovanna Coviello
Evelyne Culcay
Matteo Domeniconi
Beat Egli
Colette Fähndrich
Sebastian Fatmann
Massimo Ferrari
Hanna Fluck
Fabian Früh
Stefanie Gaube
Kaja Gebremariam
Lisa Gerlach
Dora De Giacomo
Hans Gritsch
Philippe Guillod
Samuel Henzen
Cella Hubel
Marius Hügli
Corinne Huwyler
Judith Kappes
Nadja Kobzev
Kristina Krämer
Kathrin Kunz
Petra Kupferschmid
Malin Lindholm
Alexis Luc
Stefan Maier
Adriana Pablos
Joachim Pfeffinger
Diana Pfister
Isabelle Sita Plattner
Horst Reher
Jan Rösch
Christoph Rothenhöfer
Andrea Rüegg
Christine Sander
Tanja Schmid
Jannis Schröder
Martin Schröder
Rémy Schuster
Corinne Schweizer
Stefan Segessenmann
Rebecca Silva
Chris Stephan
Irene Studer
Katrin Urwyler
Nadja Vitt
Markus Walser

Werkverzeichnis: Bauten,
Projekte und Wettbewerbe
(Auswahl)

1992

→ Umbau Terrassenvilla
am Altenberg, Bern

1994

→ Neubau Therapiepavillon,
Binningen (Wymann & Selva
Architekten)

1995

→ Umbau Bürogebäude Pirelli,
St. Jakobsstrasse, Basel

1996

→ Renovation denkmalge-
schütztes Wohnhaus Reiter-
strasse, Basel
→ Neubau Orientierungsschule
Kaltbrunnen-Schulhaus, Basel
(Wymann & Selva Architekten)
(Wettbewerb 1. Preis)

1997

→ Projektstudie Hotel
Belvedere, Interlaken

1998

→ Umbau und Renovation
Stadtvilla (Arch. R. Linder, 1898)
für Pirelli SA, Basel

2000

→ Zweistufiger Projektwettbewerb Quartierzentrum Breite,
Basel (2. Preis)
→ Zweistufiger Projektwettbewerb Tierpark Goldau, Goldau
(1. Preis)

2001

→ Neubau Doppelwohnhaus
Bäumlihof, Riehen
→ Umbau Operationssäle
für Augenklinik, Binningen
→ Erweiterung Villa V. F.,
Oberwil

2002

→ Farbkonzept Bau 15, Areal
Grenzacherstrasse,
F. Hoffmann-La Roche AG,
Basel (Arch.: O. R. Salvisberg
1936–1938)
→ Projektwettbewerb Neubau
Pädagogische Hochschule,
Goldau (3. Preis)

2003

→ Projektwettbewerb Sanierung
Bau 21, Areal Grenzacherstrasse,
F. Hoffmann-La Roche AG,
Basel (Arch.: O. R. Salvisberg
1936–1938)
→ Zweistufiger Projektwett-
bewerb Neubau Universitäts-
Kinderspital beider Basel
UKBB (5. Preis)
→ Zweistufiger städtebaulicher
Wettbewerb Landhof-Areal,
Basel (2. Preis)

2004

→ Neubau Wohnhaus beim
Wenkenpark, Riehen
→ Zweistufiger Projektwettbewerb 120 Wohnungen am Bachgraben, Allschwil (3. Preis)
→ Städtebauliche Studie Entwicklung Volta-Zentrum, Basel

2005

→ Neubau Gartenpavillon,
Allschwil
→ Neubau Wohnhaus für
Künstler, Lupsingen
→ Neubau Garderobengebäude
Sportzentrum Schützenmatte,
Basel (Wettbewerb 1. Preis)
→ Projektwettbewerb 80
Wohnungen, Zürich-Affoltern
→ Projektwettbewerb Zentrum
Guggach, 75 Wohnungen,
Zürich-Oberstrass
→ Umbau Büroräume der
Pensionskasse Basel-Stadt,
Clarastrasse, Basel
→ Erweiterung Wohnhaus B.,
Witterswil

2006

→ Erweiterung Roche Bau 41,
F. Hoffmann-La Roche AG, Basel
→ Projektwettbewerb
Wohnungen für Bern-West
→ Projekt Aufstockung Bau 21,
F. Hoffmann-La Roche AG, Basel
→ Städtebaulicher Wettbewerb
Entwicklung Gebiet Bellevue,
Kreuzlingen

2007

→ Neubau Wohnhaus am
Dorfbach, Magden
→ Bürohaus City Gate Basel,
Projekt I
→ Zweistufiger Projektwettbe-
werb Hochschule für Gestaltung
und Kunst HGK, Campus des
Bildes Dreispitz, Basel (4. Preis)

Werkverzeichnis: Bauten, Projekte und Wettbewerbe (Auswahl)

→ Sanierung Neubadschulhaus Nord, Basel
→ Sanierung Mehrfamilienhaus Rheinländerstrasse, Basel
→ Studienauftrag Altersresidenz, Lautengartenstrasse, Basel
→ Städtebauliche Planung Basel-Süd
→ Studienauftrag Mischeli, Reinach / BL

2008

→ Neubau Wohnhaus für Kunstsammler, Binningen
→ Ordos 100: Wohnhaus in der Inneren Mongolei, China
→ Ausbau Arztpraxis Laser Vista Klinik, Binningen

2009

→ Studienauftrag «Neue Durchgangsgruppe» Bürgerliches Waisenhaus, Basel
→ Studienauftrag «Luegisland», Zürich-Schwamendingen
→ Studienauftrag Neubau Mehrfamilienhaus zwischen Gerber- und Andreasstrasse, St. Gallen
→ Projektwettbewerb Neubau Verwaltungsgebäude der Stadt Biel
→ Projektwettbewerb HPS Heilpädagogische Schule Lyss
→ Projektwettbewerb Neubau Mehrfamilienhaus Areal Sandfelsen, Erlenbach (Ankauf)

2010

→ Neubau Wohnhaus S., Burggasse, Muttenz
→ Projektwettbewerb Ersatzneubau Wohnsiedlung Areal Tièchestrasse, Zürich-Wipkingen (2. Preis)
→ Umbau Einfamilienhaus S., Allschwil
→ Sanierung Apartment, Schützenmattstrasse 42, Basel
→ Studienauftrag Mehrfamilienhaus Klingelbergstrasse, Basel
→ Studienauftrag Zentrumsüberbauung Areal Hübeli, Aesch
→ Projektwettbewerb 80 Wohnungen in Reinach/BL (2. Preis)
→ Projektwettbewerb Überbauung Webi-Areal Ost, Aarburg
→ Projektstudie für Umbau und Erweiterung Wohnung 2. Obergeschoss, Gerbergässlein, Basel

2011

→ Neubau Densa-Areal: 99 Wohnungen in Basel-Nord (Projektwettbewerb 1. Preis)
→ Neubau Hofbebauung Hegenheimerstrasse, Basel (Studienauftrag 1. Preis)
→ Studienauftrag Wohnhaus Aescherstrasse, Basel
→ Projektwettbewerb Wohnungsbau Steinwiesstrasse/Irisstrasse, Zürich-Hottingen, 2011 (5. Preis)
→ Zweistufiger Projektwettbewerb Centre Communale Ville de Carouge
→ Sanierung Feuerwache Basel-Stadt, Kornhausgasse, Basel
→ Studienauftrag Ersatzneubau Luggwegstrasse, Zürich-Altstetten
→ Projektwettbewerb Ersatzneubau Wohnsiedlung im Stückler, Zürich-Altstetten
→ Studienauftrag Umbau Zolli Restaurant, Basel
→ Machbarkeitsstudie Liegenschaft Steinengraben, Vaudoise, Basel

2012

→ Gesamtsanierung Wohnhochhaus Jägerstrasse, Basel
→ Architekturbiennale Ausstellungsbeitrag; *Inside – Out by Luca Selva Architects* Palazzo Bembo, Venedig
→ Neubau Wohnhaus D., Olsberg
→ Neubau Wohnhaus mit Atelier, Burggasse, Muttenz
→ Umbau und Erweiterung Wohn- und Geschäftshaus am Marktplatz, Basel
→ Praxisausbau Laser Vista, Markthalle, Basel
→ Städtebaulicher Ideenwettbewerb Nordbahnhof, Wien
→ Projektwettbewerb Sekundarschulhaus Sandgruben, Basel (2. Preis)
→ Umbau Eingangshalle Verwaltungsgebäude Spiegelhof, Basel
→ Projektwettbewerb Neubau Marthastift, Basel (5. Preis)
→ Projektwettbewerb Ozeanium Zoo Basel (mit pool Architekten), Basel (5. Preis)
→ Studienauftrag Dychrain, Areal Läckerli Huus, Münchenstein
→ Studienauftrag Eisenbahnweg, Basel

2013

→ Neubau Generationenhaus, Binningen
→ Ersatzneubauten Wohnsiedlung, Zürich-Oerlikon (Wettbewerb 1. Preis, 1. Etappe 2013, 2. Etappe 2014)
→ Projektwettbewerb Sanierung und Modernisierung St. Jakobshalle, Basel (3. Preis)
→ Projektwettbewerb Wohnen am Park, Areal Saurer WerkZwei, Arbon (3. Preis)
→ Studienauftrag Genossenschaftliches Wohnen am Stadtrand, Bachgraben, Basel
→ Testplanung Helvetia-Campus, St. Alban-Anlage, Basel
→ Projektwettbewerb auf Einladung Wohnen im Ried-Köniz, Köniz
→ Projektwettbewerb Ersatzneubau Wohnsiedlung Seebahnstrasse, Zürich
→ Projektwettbewerb Neubau Wohnüberbauung Maiengasse, Basel (3. Preis)
→ Neubau Nachwuchs-Campus FC Basel (Studienauftrag 1. Preis)
→ Studienauftrag «Tower», Windisch
→ Sanierung Intercityhaus St. Jakobs-Strasse 3, Basel
→ Neubau Hochhaus City Gate Haus D., Basel
→ Neubau Wohnhaus M., Binningen

Laufende Projekte

→ Neubau Haus H. Rütiring, Riehen (Fertigstellung 2014)
→ Architekturbiennale Ausstellungsbeitrag; *Specific Typlogies by Luca Selva Architects* Palazzo Bembo, Venedig
→ Neubauten Areal FR Immobilien AG, Rheinfelden
→ Umbau Zentrum für Frühförderung, Elisabethenstrasse 51, Basel (Fertigstellung 2015)
→ Studienauftrag «Oberstadt», Aarburg (1. Preis)
→ Neubau Wohnüberbauung Wuhrmatt, Binningen (Studienauftrag 1. Preis, Fertigstellung 2015)
→ Neubau Wohnungen am Gellertpark, Basel (Studienauftrag 1. Preis, Fertigstellung 2015)
→ Neubau Primarschule und Sporthalle Erlenmatt, Basel (Projektwettbewerb 1. Preis, Fertigstellung 2017)
→ Neubau 135 Wohnungen Widmi 2, Lenzburg (Studienauftrag 1. Preis, Fertigstellung 2016)
→ Masterplan und Wohnbauten im KBB Kölner Baumwollquartier Holweide, Köln
→ 250 Wohnungen für Köln-Wahn
→ Aufstockung Hochhaus Bau 41, F. Hofmann-La Roche AG, Basel
→ Aufstockung Bau 35, Areal Grenzacherstrasse, F. Hofmann-La Roche AG, Basel

Selected List
Buildings, Projects
and Competitions

1992

→ Remodeling, Terraced Villa, Bern-Altenberg

1994

→ New Building, Therapy Pavilion, Binningen (Wymann & Selva Architects)

1995

→ Remodeling, Pirelli Office Building, St. Jakobsstrasse, Basel

1996

→ Renovation, Heritage-listed House, Reiterstrasse, Basel
→ New Building, *Orientierungsschule* [grades 5–6], Kaltbrunnen School, Basel (Wymann & Selva Architects) (Competition, 1st Prize)

1997

→ Project Study, Belvedere Hotel, Interlaken

1998

→ Remodeling and Renovation, City Villa (Arch.: R. Linder, 1898), Pirelli SA, Basel

2000

→ Two-Stage Project Competition, Breite Neighborhood Center, Basel (2nd Prize)
→ Two-Stage Project Competition. Goldau Animal Park, Goldau (1st Prize)

2001

→ New Building, Bäumlihof Duplex, Riehen
→ Remodeling, Eye Clinic Operating Rooms, Binningen
→ Extension, Villa V. F., Oberwil

2002

→ Color Concept, Building 15, Grenzacherstrasse Premises, F. Hoffmann-La Roche & Cie AG, Basel (Arch.: O. R. Salvisberg, 1936–1938)
→ Project Competition, New Building, Schwyz University of Teacher Education, Goldau (3rd Prize)

2003

→ Project Competition, Refurbishment, Building 21, Grenzacherstrasse Premises, F. Hoffmann-La Roche & Cie AG, Basel (Arch.: O. R. Salvisberg 1936–1938)
→ Two-Stage Project Competition, New Building, University Children's Hospital Basel UKBB (5th Prize)
→ Two-Stage Competition, Urban Development, Landhof Grounds, Basel (2nd Prize)

2004

→ New Building, House at Wenkenpark, Riehen
→ Two-Stage Project Competition, 120 Apartments at Bachgraben, Allschwil (3rd Prize)
→ Urban Development Planning Study, Volta Center, Basel

2005

→ New Building, Garden Pavilion, Allschwil
→ New Building, House for Artists, Lupsingen
→ New Building, Changing Rooms, Schützenmatte Sports Center, Basel (Competition, 1st Prize)
→ Project Competition, 80 Apartments, Zurich-Affoltern
→ Project Competition, 75 Apartments, Guggach Center, Zurich-Oberstrass
→ Remodeling, Office Space, Basel-City Employees Pension Fund, Clarastrasse, Basel
→ Extension, House B., Witterswil

2006

→ Extension, Building 41, F. Hoffmann-La Roche & Cie AG, Basel
→ Additional Story Project, Housing, Bern-West
→ Additional Story Project, Building 21, F. Hoffmann-La Roche & Cie AG, Basel
→ Urban Development Competition, Bellevue Area, Kreuzlingen

2007

→ New Building, House at Dorfbach, Magden
→ Phase I, City Gate Office Building, Basel
→ Two-Stage Project Competition, Academy of Art and Design (HGK), Dreispitz Campus of the Image, Basel (4th Prize)
→ Refurbishment, Neubad Schoolhouse North, Basel
→ Refurbishment, Multiunit Residential Building, Rheinländerstrasse, Basel
→ Study Commission, Senior Citizens Residence, Lautengartenstrasse, Basel
→ Urban Planning, Basel-South
→ Study Commission, Mischeli, Reinach/BL

2008

→ New Building, House for Art Collectors, Binningen
→ Ordos 100, Residential Building, Inner Mongolia, China
→ Expansion, Medical Practice, Laser Vista Clinic, Binningen

2009

→ Study Commission, *Neue Durchgangsgruppe* [Children & Young Adults Crisis Center], Municipal Orphanage, Basel
→ Study Commission, Luegisland, Zurich-Schwamendingen
→ Study Commission, New Building, Multiunit Residential Building, Gerber- & Andreasstrasse, St. Gallen
→ Project Competition, New Building, Administration Facilities, City of Biel
→ Project Competition, *Heilpädagogische Schule HPS* [Remedial Education College], Lyss
→ Project Competition, New Building, Multiunit Residential Building, Sandfelsen Area, Erlenbach (Acquisition)

2010

→ New Building, House S., Burggasse, Muttenz
→ Project Competition, New Replacement Building, Tièchestrasse Area Residential Settlement, Zurich-Wipkingen (2nd Prize)
→ Remodeling, Single Family House S., Allschwil
→ Refurbishment, Apartment Suite, Schützenmattstrasse 42, Basel
→ Study Commission, Multiunit Residential Building, Klingelbergstrasse, Basel
→ Study Commission, Hub Redevelopment, Hübeli Area, Aesch
→ Project Competition, 80 Apartments, Reinach/BL (2nd Prize)
→ Project Competition, Redevelopment, Webi Area East, Aarburg
→ Project Study, Remodeling & Expansion, Apartment 2nd Floor, Gerbergässlein, Basel

2011

→ New Building, Densa-Areal, 99 Apartments, Basel-North (Project Competition, 1st Prize)
→ New Building, Hegenheimerstrasse Backstreet Multiunit Residence, Basel (Study Commission, 1st Prize)
→ Study Commission, Residential Building, Aescherstrasse, Basel
→ Project Competition, Apartment Building, Steinwies- & Irisstrasse, Zurich-Hottingen, (5th Prize)
→ Two-stage Project Competition, Centre Communale, Ville de Carouge
→ Remodeling, Basel-City Fire Station, Kornhausgasse, Basel
→ Study Commission, New Replacement Building, Luggwegstrasse, Zurich-Altstetten
→ Project Competition, New Replacement Building, Im Stückler Residential Settlement, Zurich-Altstetten
→ Study Commission, Remodeling, Zolli Restaurant, Basel
→ Feasibility Study, Steinengraben Property, Vaudoise, Basel

2012

→ Total Refurbishment, Residential High-Rise, Jägerstrasse, Basel
→ Exhibition Contribution, *Inside – Out by Luca Selva Architects,* Venice Biennale of Architecture, Palazzo Bembo, Venice
→ New Building, House D., Olsberg
→ New Building, House with Studio, Burggasse, Muttenz
→ Remodeling and Expansion, Residential & Office Building, Marktplatz, Basel

→ Expansion, Medical Practice, Laser Vista, Markthalle, Basel
→ Competition, Urban Planning Ideas, Nordbahnhof [North Station], Vienna
→ Project Competition, Sandgruben Secondary Schoolhouse, Basel (2nd Prize)
→ Remodeling, Entrance Hall, Spiegelhof City Administration Building, Basel
→ Project Competition, New Building, Marthastift, Basel (5th Prize)
→ Project Competition, Oceanium, Basel Zoo (in collaboration with pool Architects), Basel (5th Prize)
→ Study Commission, Dychrain, Läckerli Huus Area, Münchenstein
→ Study Commission, Eisenbahnweg, Basel

2013

→ New Building, Generational House, Binningen
→ New Replacement Building, Residential Settlement, Zurich-Oerlikon (Competition, 1st Prize, 1st stage 2013, 2nd stage 2014)
→ Project Competition, Remodeling and Modernization, St. Jakobshalle, Basel (3rd Prize)
→ Competition, *Wohnen am Park* [Dwelling at the Park], Saurer WerkZwei Area, Arbon (3rd Prize)
→ Study Commission, Cooperative Housing at the Periphery, Bachgraben, Basel
→ Test Planning, Helvetia Campus, St. Alban Facilities, Basel
→ Project Competition by Invitation, Housing in Ried-Köniz, Köniz
→ Project Competition, New Replacement Building, Seebahnstrasse Residential Settlement, Zurich
→ Project Competition, New Building, Residential Complex, Maiengasse, Basel (3rd Prize)
→ New Building, Youngster Campus FC Basel (Study Commission 1st Prize)
→ Study Commission, "Tower," Windisch
→ Reburbishment, Intercityhaus, St. Jakobs-Strasse 3, Basel
→ New Building, High-Rise, City Gate Building D., Basel
→ New Building, House M., Binningen

Current Projects

→ New Building, House H., Rütiring, Riehen (Completion 2014)
→ Exhibition Contribution, *Specific Typologies by Luca Selva Architects*, Venice Biennale of Architecture, Palazzo Bembo, Venice
→ New Buildings, FR Immobilien AG Area, Rheinfelden
→ Remodeling, Center for Early Intervention, Elisabethenstrasse 51, Basel (Completion 2015)
→ Study Commission, "Oberstadt," Aarburg (1st Prize)
→ New Building, Wuhrmatt Residential Complex, Binningen (Study Commission 1st Prize, Completion 2015)
→ New Apartment Building at Gellertpark, Basel (Study Commission 1st Prize, Completion 2015)
→ New Building, Erlenmatt Primary School and Gym, Basel (Project Competition, 1st Prize, Completion 2017)
→ New 135-unit Apartment Building, Widmi 2, Lenzburg (Study Commission, 1st Prize, Completion 2016)
→ Master Plan and Housing Complex, KBB Kölner Baumwollquartier [Former Cotton Factory Quarter], Cologne-Holweide
→ 250 Apartments, Cologne-Wahn
→ High-Rack Warehouse Story Addition and Façade Refurbishment, Building 41, F. Hoffmann-La Roche AG, Basel
→ Story Addition, Building 35, F. Hoffmann-La Roche AG, Basel

Impressum
Imprint

Herausgeber und Texte:
Editor and Texts:
Christoph Wieser, Zürich

Konzept und Mitarbeit:
Concept and Collaboration:
Luca Selva Architekten, Basel;
Projektleitung:
Project Manager:
Petra Waldburger

Konzept und Gestaltung:
Concept and Graphic Design
Bonbon – Valeria Bonin,
Diego Bontognali, Zürich

Lektorat deutsch:
Editing German:
Karoline Mueller-Stahl, Leipzig

Übersetzung:
Translation:
Linda Cassens Stoian, Basel

Lektorat englisch:
Editing English:
Andrew Horsfield, Wien

Korrektorat deutsch und englisch:
Proofreading German and English:
Lisa Schons, Zürich

Lithografie, Druck und Bindung:
Lithography, Printing and Binding:
DZA Druckerei zu Altenburg GmbH, Altenburg, Thüringen

© 2014 Park Books, Zürich und Christoph Wieser
© 2014 Park Books, Zurich, and Christoph Wieser

© für die Texte: die Autoren
© for the texts: the authors

Für die Werke von Candida Höfer und Thomas Ruff:
© 2014, ProLitteris, Zürich
For the works by Candida Höfer and Thomas Ruff:
© 2014, ProLitteris, Zürich

Bild C, S. 41
Mikael Bergquist und Olof Michélsen (Hrsg.), *Josef Frank. Architektur*, Basel/Boston/Berlin: Birkhäuser Verlag 1995, S. 83.
Picture C, p. 41
Mikael Bergquist and Olof Michélsen (eds.), *Josef Frank. Architektur* (Basel/Boston/Berlin: Birkhäuser Verlag 1995), 83.

Bild H, S. 45
Rafael Diez und Kenneth Frampton, "José Antonio Coderch. Houses", in: *2G*, Nr. 33, 2005, S. 37.
Picture H, p. 45
Rafael Diez and Kenneth Frampton, "José Antonio Coderch. Houses," in: *2G*, no. 33, 2005, 37.

© für die Fotografien: siehe Projektlegenden
© for the photographs: see project captions

Park Books
Niederdorfstrasse 54
8001 Zürich
Schweiz/Switzerland
www.park-books.com

Alle Rechte vorbehalten; kein Teil dieses Werks darf in irgendeiner Form ohne vorherige schriftliche Genehmigung des Verlags reproduziert oder unter Verwendung elektronischer Systeme verarbeitet, vervielfältigt oder verbreitet werden.

All rights reserved; no part of this publication may be reproduced, stored in a retrieval system or transmitted in any form or by any means, electronic, mechanical, photocopying, recording or otherwise, without the prior written consent of the publisher.

ISBN 978-3-906027-56-2

5A

5B

5 C

|—————| 5 m

5D

5E

Wohnhaus mit Atelier
Muttenz, 2010–2012

House with Studio
Muttenz, 2010–2012

Von der dreieckigen Eingangshalle führt ein sich konisch ausweitender Korridor ins halbgeschossig abgetiefte Atelier. Es ist unterirdisch angelegt und durch vier grosse, prismatische Oberlichtkörper in rauer Betonstruktur taghell belichtet, die im Garten wie zufällig platzierte Objekte erscheinen. Das Haus selbst legt sich auf zwei Seiten als Futteral um das Atelier. Während die hangseitige Rückwand in einer geraden Linie verläuft und nahezu geschlossen ist, entfalten sich die repräsentativen Räume auf der Aussichtsseite zu einer im Grundriss wie im Schnitt vielgestaltigen Wohnlandschaft polygonaler Ausprägung.

Die Zonierung des weitgehend als Einraumhaus konzipierten Gebäudes erfolgt einerseits mittels Einschnürungen und Ausweitungen, andererseits über Treppenstufen. So führt die *promenade architecturale* vom Eingang über eine mehrfach abgewinkelte Treppe am Gäste- und Schlafbereich vorbei ins Wohngeschoss. Dieses ist parallel zum Hang in die Küche, einen kleinen Innenhof und das Esszimmer gegliedert. Den Abschluss macht eine Pergola in Sichtbeton, die als Bindglied zwischen Innenraum und Garten vermittelt. Quer zum Hang führen breiter werdende Stufen in den Wohnraum hinauf, an dessen Ende sich ein grosses Aussichtsfenster und das Cheminée die gefaltete Stirnwand teilen. Das Aufwärtsschreiten im Kontrast zum Geländeverlauf weckt ein vergleichbares Gefühl wie in der Villa Malaparte auf Capri, wo man über ebenfalls konisch zulaufende Stufen auf das Dach des Hauses gelangt. Hier im Wohnraum dieses Hauses mit Atelier steht man erhaben in Bezug zur Umgebung und wähnt sich deshalb eher auf einem Deck denn in einem geschlossenen Raum. Die Materialisierung ist innen und aussen zurückhaltend elegant, einzig die in Sand verlegten grossformatigen Steinplatten der Böden sowie die von den Bewohnern teils farbig interpretierten Wände setzen Akzente.

Auf der benachbarten Parzelle steht ein weiteres Einfamilienhaus von Luca Selva Architekten, das Wohnhaus S. (2010). Im äusseren Ausdruck ähnlich, ist es aber völlig anders strukturiert: Parallel zum Hang verlaufen drei unterschiedlich lange Raumschichten, die im Schnitt abgetreppt sind. Dadurch entsteht dort über die Diagonale eine spannungsreiche Abfolge der Wohnräume mit dem Cheminéezimmer als Zentrum.

From the triangular entrance hall a conically widening corridor leads to the half-story-embedded studio. Laid out subterraneously, it is exposed to broad daylight by four large prismatic skylights-executed as raw concrete structures, which in the garden appear like randomly placed objects. The house itself retracts on two sides, sheath-like, around the studio. While the slope-side back wall proceeds in a straight line and is almost closed, the representative spaces unfold on the side with a view to create a multifaceted dwelling landscape shaped as a polygon in ground plan as well as section.

The zoning of this building, which is mainly conceived as a one room house, occurs, on the one hand, via constricting and widening out and, on the other hand, through stairs. Thereby the *promenade architecturale* leads from the entrance over a multi-angled flight of stairs past the guest and sleeping areas up to the living space level. Located parallel to the slope, this level is divided into kitchen, small inner courtyard and dining room. Concluding the sequence is an exposed concrete pergola that functions as a connecting element between interior and garden. Situated perpendicular to the slope, widening steps lead up to the living room at whose end there is a large panorama window and fireplace, which share the folded front wall. The striding upwards in contrast to the layout of the terrain evokes a similar sensation as Villa Malaparte on Capri where, likewise, conically tapering steps lead up to the roof of the house. Here in the living room of House with Studio one stands elevated in relation to the surroundings and therefore fancies oneself to be on a deck rather than in a closed space. Inside and out the materialization is elegantly understated except for the accentuating flooring with large-format stone slabs laid in sand and some colorful walls, interpreted by the clients themselves.

On the neighboring plot stands another single family house by Luca Selva Architects, House S. (2010). While similar-looking from the outside, it is structured completely differently. Parallel to the slope there are three layers of rooms with different lengths which are stepped in section. There this results in a fascinating sequence of living spaces running across the diagonal with a fireplace parlor as center.

Mitarbeit: Alex Pipoz
Tragwerksplanung: Beurret Ingenieure GmbH, Basel
Fotos: Ruedi Walti

Staff: Alex Pipoz
Structural Engineering: Beurret Ingenieure GmbH, Basel
Photos: Ruedi Walti

5F

5G

5H

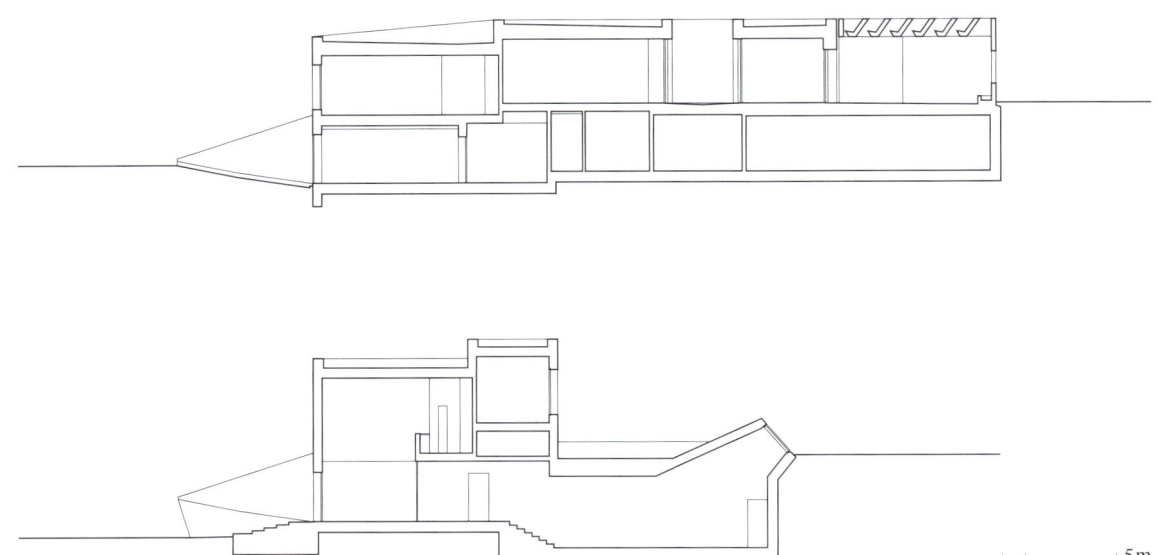

6A

6B

6 C

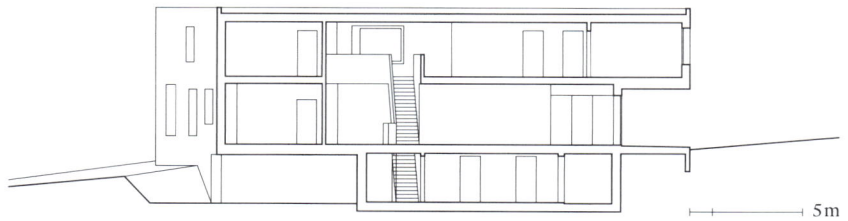

5 m

6 D

Wohnhaus für Kunstsammler
Binningen, 2006–2008

House for Art Collectors
Binningen, 2006–2008

Die Architektur als Rahmen für ein Leben mit Kunst, wobei das Haus Hintergrund und selbstbewusster Akteur sein soll: Diese Vorgabe der Bauherrschaft prägt den Entwurf von der Wegführung, der Grösse und Proportionierung der Räume über die Ausbildung der Öffnungen bis hin zur Materialisierung. Das Erdgeschoss, in dem hauptsächlich die grossformatigen Fotografien zeitgenössischer Künstler, jahrzehntealte Kakteen und antike Figuren platziert sind, ist in eine vielgestaltige Raumsequenz gegliedert. Ein honigfarbener Stampflehmboden des Vorarlberger Lehmbauspezialisten Martin Rauch →78 führt vom Eingangsbereich über den sich ausweitenden Korridor zur zweigeschossigen Halle und von dort in den Wohnraum.

    Archaisch und gleichsam wie ein kostbarer Teppich wirkt der Boden mit seiner variierenden Oberfläche. Damit kontrastiert er aufs Schönste die industriell gefertigten Aluminiumprofile der Schiebefenster, welche die Passage von der Halle zum Wohnraum räumlich einschnüren, gegen den Garten hin aber grossflächig öffnen. An dieser Stelle befindet sich der eingezogene Sitzplatz und im Obergeschoss eine Galerie, die über ein Binnenfenster Wohnraum und Halle verbindet. Hier kulminiert die Durchdringung von Innen- und Aussenraum und es wird klar, weshalb Äusseres wie Inneres in Weiss gehalten sind: Der winkelförmige Grundriss rückt immer wieder Innen- und Aussenwände gleichzeitig ins Blickfeld. Indem die Öffnungen innenbündig angeschlagen und in derselben Farbe wie die Wände gestrichen sind, fällt die Umgebung in den Innenraum ein, wirkt bildartig und tritt damit in lebhafte Beziehung zu den Exponaten.

    Der Verputz aus Carrara-Marmor verleiht dem Gebäude strahlend weisse Oberflächen. Im Brennpunkt der mehrfach abgewinkelten Südwestfassade liegt das Schwimmbad, objekthaft und wie eine Kostbarkeit im orangeroten Hartgummibelag platziert. Sorgfältig mit ausgesuchten Pflanzen gestaltet, ergänzt der Garten «61 das Wohnhaus auf ebenso eigenständige wie stimmungsvolle Weise.

Architecture as the frame for a life with art, whereby the house should be background and self-aware protagonist: these pre-specifications of the clients shaped the design process from circulation, size and proportioning of the spaces to articulation of the openings as well as materialization. The ground floor, where mainly large-format photography by contemporary artists, decades-old cacti and antique sculptures are located, is divided into a multifarious spatial sequence. A honey-colored rammed earth floor by the Vorarlberg loam building specialist Martin Rauch →78 leads from the entrance area across the widening corridor to a double-story hall and further on into the living room.

    The floor appears archaic and at the same time like an expensive carpet with its varying surface. Thereby it contrasts wonderfully with the industrial-fabricated aluminum profiles of the sliding windows, which spatially constrict the passage from the hall to the living room but open extensively towards the garden. At this spot there is a withdrawn seating area and, on the upper story, a gallery connecting living room and hall via an inner window. Here the fusion of interior and exterior space culminates and it becomes clear why outside as well as inside are kept white: again and again the L-shaped ground plan shifts interior and exterior walls into the field of vision. Because the openings are mounted flush with the inner wall and painted the same color as the walls, the exterior environment seems to invade the inner space, appears image-like and thereby enters into an animated dialogue with the exhibited artworks.

    The plaster executed with Carrara marble provides the building with gleaming white surfaces. At the focal point of the multi-angled southwest façade lies the swimming pool, object-like and placed in the surrounding orange-red hard rubber flooring like a precious object. Carefully embellished with select plants, the garden «61 complements the dwelling in an autonomous as well as ambient way.

Mitarbeit: Barbara Andres, Roger Braccini
Bauleitung: Architekturbüro Raymond Richner
Landschaftsarchitektur: August + Margrith Künzel Landschaftsarchitekten AG, Basel
Tragwerksplanung: Walther Mory Maier Bauingenieure AG, Basel
Fotos: HG Esch (A–H, J–M), Ruedi Walti (J)

Staff: Barbara Andres, Roger Braccini
Construction Management: Architekturbüro Raymond Richner
Landscape Architecture: August + Margrith Künzel Landschaftsarchitekten AG, Basel
Structural Engineering: Walther Mory Maier Bauingenieure AG, Basel
Photos: HG Esch (A–H, J–M), Ruedi Walti (J)

Der Stampflehmboden
Martin Rauch

Rammed Earth Floor
Martin Rauch

Dem Fussboden wird im Vergleich zu seinem eigentlichen Stellenwert im Allgemeinen viel zu wenig Beachtung geschenkt. Materialität und Ästhetik der Fussböden wirken sich enorm auf den Innenraum als Ganzen aus und beeinflussen das Raumgefühl entscheidend. Dieser Umstand zeigt sich beim Wohnhaus für Kunstsammler in Binningen besonders deutlich. Als wäre er immer schon dagewesen, zieht sich der Stampflehmboden durch das Erdgeschoss. Ein archaischer Kontrast zu dem weissen, lichtdurchfluteten Raumgefüge, das an sich bereits einen besonderen Ort für die ausgestellten Kunstwerke schafft.

Lehm entsteht bei der Verwitterung oder beim Zerfall von Gesteinsschichten infolge von geologischen Vorgängen und Erosionseinflüssen zum Beispiel durch Wasser, Frost, Wind oder Temperaturwechsel. Die so entstandenen Verwitterungsreste werden vorwiegend durch Wasser, aber auch Wind (Löss) verfrachtet und abgelagert. Unser Planet ist durch Erosion nachhaltig geprägt und deshalb ist Lehm auch überall vorhanden und nutzbar. Lehme sind je nach Fundort sehr verschieden. Der Anteil an Ton, Schluff, Sand und Kies variiert. Diese Anteilsverhältnisse bestimmen oft die örtlich unterschiedlichen historischen Lehmbauweisen. Auch die Grundfarbe dieser Lehme ist regional sehr verschieden.

Beim Wohnhaus für Kunstsammler wurde Lehm mit Schotter vorgemischt, als krümelige, erdfeuchte Masse in «Big Bags» auf die Baustelle geliefert und per Schubkarre in das Hausinnere transportiert. Auf eine druckstabile Wärmedämmung wurden Fussboden-Heizleitungen verlegt und mit einem weichen Lehm-Sand-Gemisch eingemörtelt. Im Anschluss wurde die oben genannte Lehmmischung ca. 14 Zentimeter hoch eingefüllt, sorgfältig abgezogen und mit Rüttelplatten auf 10 Zentimeter Höhe verdichtet. Nach dem Austrocknen erfolgte eine Versiegelung mit Wachs. Das Einbringen, Verdichten und die Oberflächenbehandlung sind eine vielschichtige Prozedur, die mehrere Arbeitsgänge beinhaltet und durch handwerkliche Intensität und Sensibilität eine entsprechende Qualität erreicht. Da Stampflehmböden keine Eigenspannung aufweisen, sind sie fugenlos ausführbar und können wie hier auch über mehrere Räume fliessend eingebaut werden. Jeder hergestellte Lehmboden ist auf seine Weise ein Unikat, die ihm jeweils eigene Charakteristik ist zumeist nicht wiederholbar.

Es war uns ein Anliegen, dass die Bewohner des Kunstsammlerhauses, wie alle unsere Kunden, im Vorfeld Referenzprojekte besichtigen. Denn nur so kann vermieden werden, dass falsche Erwartungen in einen Lehmboden gesetzt werden. Stark beanspruchte Stellen, zum Beispiel in Türdurchgängen oder bei Sitzplätzen, können eine natürliche Abnützung zur Folge haben. Diese kleineren Beschädigungen – und das ist ein wesentlicher Vorteil des Lehms – sind gut reparierbar. Mit regelmässiger Pflege lassen sich solche Abnutzungen ausserdem verringern beziehungsweise sogar vermeiden. Grundsätzlich sind Stampflehmböden ähnlich belastbar wie geölte oder gewachste Holzböden, und wie diese sind sie auch zu benutzen und zu pflegen.

Considering its actual significance, generally far too little attention is paid to the floor, whose materiality and aesthetic have an enormous effect on interior space as a whole and decisively influence the feel of a room. This fact is particularly evident at House for Art Collectors in Binningen. As if it had always been there, the rammed earth floor extends throughout the ground level, an archaic contrast to the white, flooded-with-light spatial sequence, which in itself already creates an extraordinary place for the exhibited artworks.

Loam is created when rock layers weather or decompose as a result of geological processes and the influence of erosion, e.g., as caused by water, frost, wind or temperature fluctuations. The weathered remains of this process are mainly carried and deposited by water, but also wind (loess). Erosion has had a lasting impact on our planet, which is why loam can be found and used everywhere. Loam differs depending on the site of excavation. The amount of clay, silt, sand and gravel varies. These proportional relationships often define the locally different traditional loam building techniques. Also the color of this loam changes greatly from region to region.

At House for Art Collectors clay was pre-mixed with gravel, delivered in "Big Bags" to the construction site as a crumbly, soil-damp mass and hauled into the house with wheelbarrows. Underfloor heating pipes were installed on a pressure-resistant thermal insulation layer and mortared in place with a supple loam-sand mixture. Finally the abovementioned mixture was filled in about 14 cm high, carefully screeded and then rammed or compacted to a height of 10 cm with air compression beaters and vibration rolls. After drying, the floor was sealed with wax. Installation, compacting and surface treatment are a multifaceted procedure that involves several stages of work and achieves a respective level of quality through the intensity and sensitivity of the craftsmanship. Because rammed earth floors have no internal stress, they can be laid without seams and, as at House for Art Collectors, be installed flowing across several spaces. Every earth floor produced is unique in its own way, i.e., the qualities creating its distinguishing character cannot for the most part be reproduced.

It was important to us that the inhabitants of House for Art Collectors, like all our clients, would visit reference projects in advance. That is the only way to avoid false expectations concerning earth floors. Heavily used spots, e.g., doorways or seating areas can show normal wear and tear. These slight damages – and that is one of the main advantages of loam – are easy to repair. Regular maintenance can minimize or even avoid this kind of abrasion. Basically rammed earth floors are as durable as oiled or waxed wooden floors and can be used and maintained just like them.

6E

6F

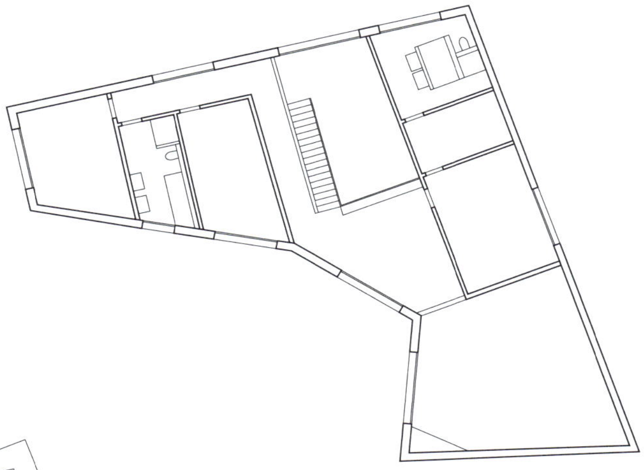

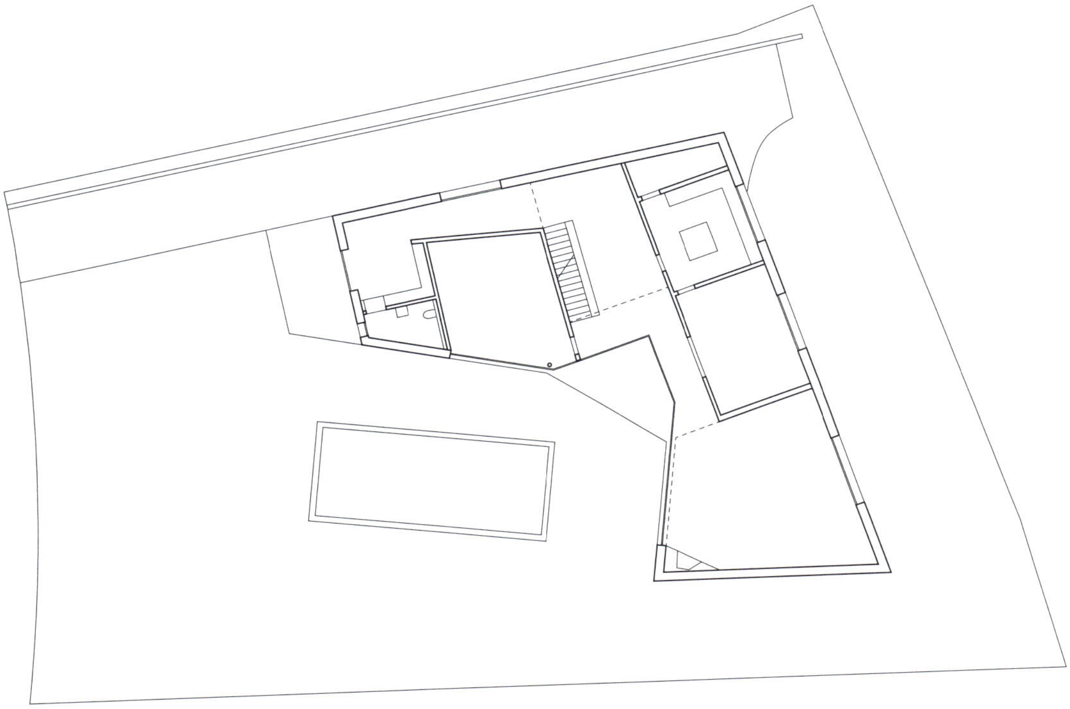

80

6 G

6H

6I

6 J

6 K

6 L

6 M

7 A

7C

7B

7D

Wohnhaus M.
Binningen, 2011–2013

House M.
Binningen, 2011–2013

Das Wohnhaus M. ist eine typologische Weiterentwicklung des Wohnhauses für Kunstsammler «75: Indem das winkelförmige Volumen hier zu einem Hufeisen ergänzt wurde, ergibt sich ein dreiseitig gefasster Hofraum. An dessen engster Stelle liegt – wie beim Kunstsammlerhaus – der vom Obergeschoss überdeckte, in die Volumetrie eingezogene Sitzplatz. Während das Erdgeschoss als offen fliessende Raumsequenz einen hohen Öffentlichkeitsgrad aufweist, befinden sich im Obergeschoss eine Reihe abgetrennter Räume. Das Schlafzimmer der Eltern ist als mehrteilige Suite mit dazugehöriger Terrasse angelegt, die als südländisch anmutendes Aussenzimmer mit Öffnungen in den Wänden gestaltet ist und deshalb von der Strasse her als Teil der Volumetrie erscheint.

Im Parterre bilden die zentralen Aufenthaltsbereiche an den beiden Kopfenden der Gebäudeflügel die räumlichen Schwerpunkte. Befindet sich im kürzeren Flügel das der Küche vorgelagerte Esszimmer, ist es auf der gegenüberliegenden Seite der Wohnraum. Dank der präzisen Setzung verschiedener Öffnungstypen ergeben sich teils überraschende Durchblicke, etwa vom Essbereich über den Hof durch das Fernsehzimmer wieder nach draussen oder von der Küche via Binnenfenster und Essraum in den Garten. Als räumlich spektakuläre Verbindung vom Garageneingang bis in das Schlafgeschoss ist die rund neun Meter hohe Treppenhalle angelegt. Weiss gestrichen wie alle Wände und Decken, entwickelt sie einen starken vertikalen Sog.

Deutlicher noch als bei anderen Wohnbauten von Luca Selva Architekten ist das Schwimmbad Teil der volumetrischen Gesamtkomposition. Hier wird die Bodenplatte in die Umgebung verlängert und verortet neben dem Wasserbecken eine Pergola samt Aussentoilette und Abstellfläche.

Typologically, House M. is a further development of House for Art Collectors «75. Here amplifying the angled volume into a horseshoe shape creates a three-sided, contained courtyard. At its narrowest part — as at House for Art Collectors — there is a seating area withdrawn into the volumetry and sheltered by the upper story. While the openly flowing spatial sequence of the ground floor evidences a high degree of publicness, on the upper story there is a series of partitioned spaces. The parents' bedroom is laid out as a suite with several parts including a terrace, which is designed as a Mediterranean-style exterior room with openings in the walls making it appears as part of the volumetry when seen from the street.

The main living areas are located in the parterre at both head ends of the building's wings and constitute spatial focal points. While the shorter wing contains a dining area situated in front of the kitchen, the opposite side is defined by a living room. The precise setting of different opening types offers occasionally surprising through-views, e.g., from the dining area across the courtyard through the TV room and again towards the exterior, or from the kitchen via an inner window and dining area into the garden. The nearly-nine-meter-high stair hall is designed as a spatially spectacular connection, leading from the garage entrance up to the sleeping level. Painted white like all the other walls and ceilings, the vertical pull is intensified.

Even more pronounced than in other residential buildings by Luca Selva Architects, the swimming pool is unmistakably part of the overall volumetric composition. The foundation slab has been extended into the environment outdoors, and in addition to serving as the foundation for the water basin, it provides the base for a pergola including an outside bathroom and storage area.

Mitarbeit: Véronique Caviezel, Jonathan Benhamu
Bauleitung: Architekturbüro Raymond Richner
Tragwerksplanung: Schnetzer Puskas Ingenieure AG, Basel
Fotos: Yohan Zerdoun

Staff: Véronique Caviezel, Jonathan Benhamu
Construction Management: Architekturbüro Raymond Richner
Structural Engineering: Schnetzer Puskas Ingenieure AG, Basel
Photos: Yohan Zerdoun

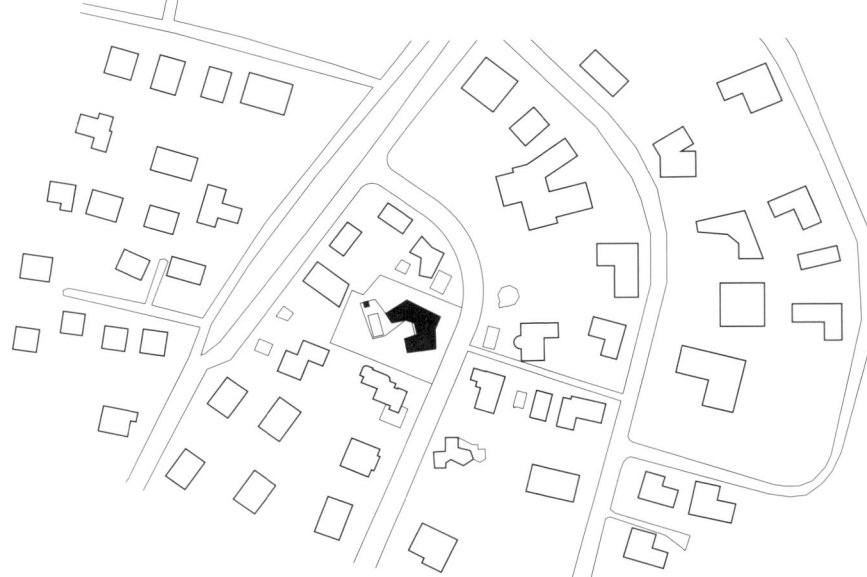

7E

7F

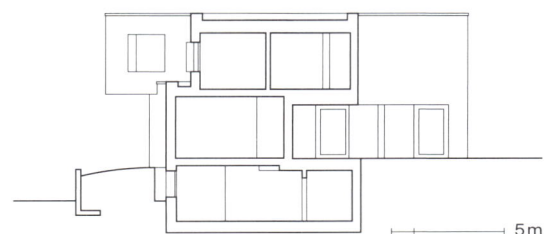

5m

7G

7H

7I

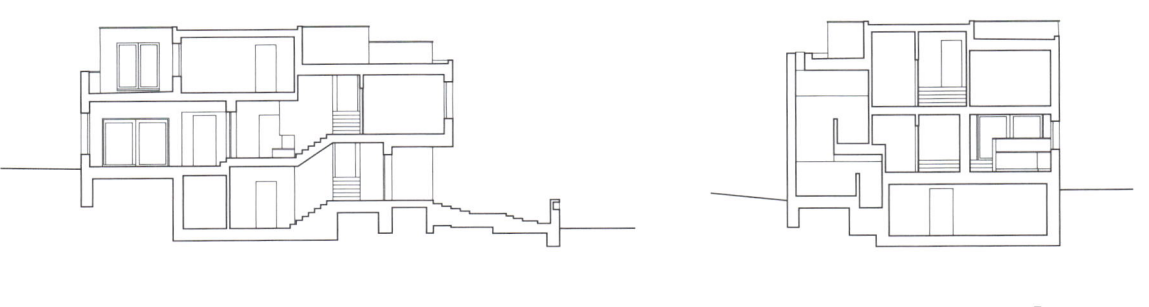

8 A

5 m

8 B

8 C

8 D

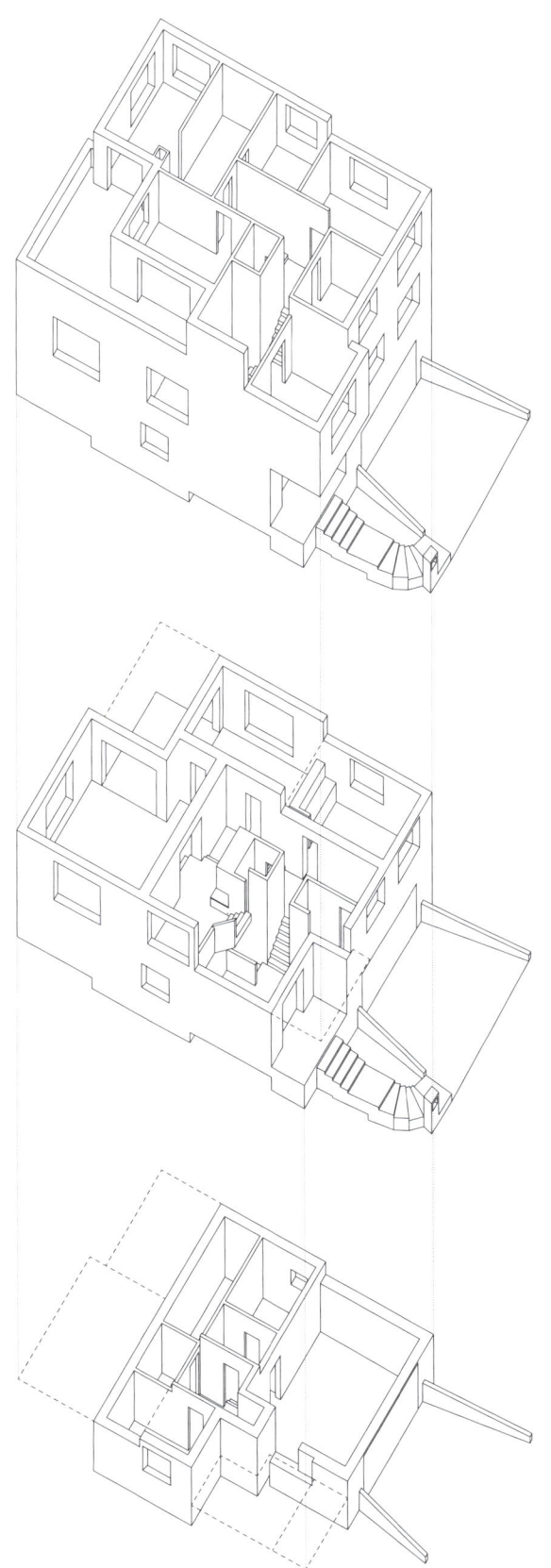

8 E

Haus H.
Riehen, 2012–2014

House H.
Riehen, 2012–2014

Zentrales Element des Haus H. mit seiner Raumplanstruktur ist das attraktive, vielgestaltige Treppenhaus. Den unteren Auftakt bildet im Garagengeschoss ein kleiner Vorraum, von dem man in die halbgeschossig versetzte Eingangshalle gelangt, die dank lateral angeordnetem, zweigeschossigem Luftraum trotz knapper Fläche grosszügig wirkt. Spiralförmig windet sich die Treppe nach oben, deren unterschiedlich breite und verschieden lange Läufe von Zwischenpodesten unterbrochen sind, von denen aus die einzelnen Räume erschlossen werden. Auf die Eingangshalle folgt die Küche und von dort gelangt man über einige Stufen in den erhöhten Essbereich, der übereck mit dem Wohnraum verbunden ist. Diesem vorgelagert ist das Cheminée als atmosphärisches Zentrum des Treppenhauses. Dazu gehört ein Vorplatz mit Sichtbezug zum Eingang hinunter – eine Konstellation, die ein wenig an die Halle eines Landhauses denken lässt. Das Oberlichtband des Treppenhauses taucht die Aussenwand in Tageslicht und reflektiert dieses bis ins Innere des Gebäudes, wo nach einer letzten 90-Grad-Drehung und einem abschliessenden Podest das oberste Geschoss des Hauses erreicht ist.

Gegen aussen manifestiert sich der Raumplan in ungewohnt zueinander versetzten Öffnungen und einigen Vor- und Rücksprüngen der Fassaden; sie brechen das kompakte Volumen auf und bereichern es. Auch dieses Haus ist innen und aussen weiss gestrichen, wobei die leicht unregelmässige Oberfläche des Verputzes das Gebäude massiver erscheinen lässt, als es wegen der Aussendämmung tatsächlich ist.

Mitarbeit: Véronique Caviezel
Tragwerksplanung: Beurret Ingenieure GmbH, Basel
Fotos: Yohan Zerdoun

The central element of House H. with its *Raumplan* structure is the attractive, multifaceted stairwell. The lower prelude begins in a small vestibule at the garage level then leads to the half-story-raised entrance hall where the laterally-arranged, two-story open air space appears generous despite the scant surface area. The staircase spirals upward; the different widths and various lengths of its flights are interrupted by intermediate landings providing access to the rooms. Past the entrance hall is the kitchen and from there a couple of steps lead up to the elevated dining area, which is connected to the living room around a corner. In front is the fireplace, the atmospheric center of the stairwell. Complementing this feature is a foyer landing with a visual connection to the entrance below – a constellation that is somewhat reminiscent of the hall in a country manor. The strip of skylights in the stairwell floods daylight onto the outer wall, which reflects this illumination deep into the interior of the building where, after a last 90-degree turn and final landing, the top level has been reached.

From the outside the *Raumplan* becomes manifest in the unconventionally staggered openings and some projections and setbacks of the façades which disrupt and enrich the compact volume. This house, as well, is painted white inside and out, although the slightly irregular surface of the plaster makes the building appear more massive than it is due to the exterior insulation.

Staff: Véronique Caviezel
Structural Engineering: Beurret Ingenieure GmbH, Basel
Photos: Adriano A. Biondo, Yohan Zerdoun

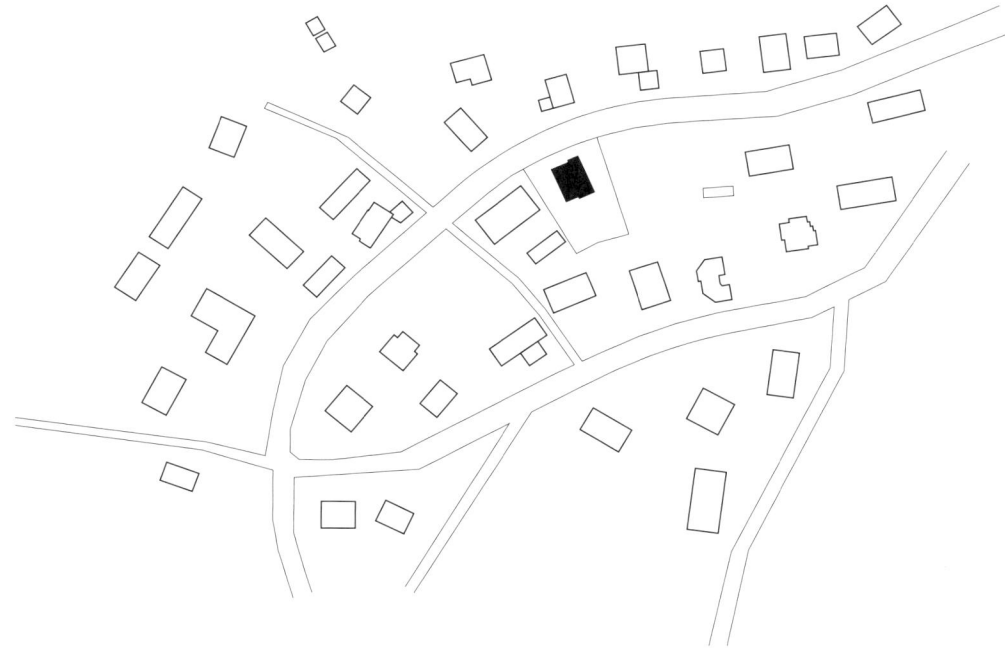

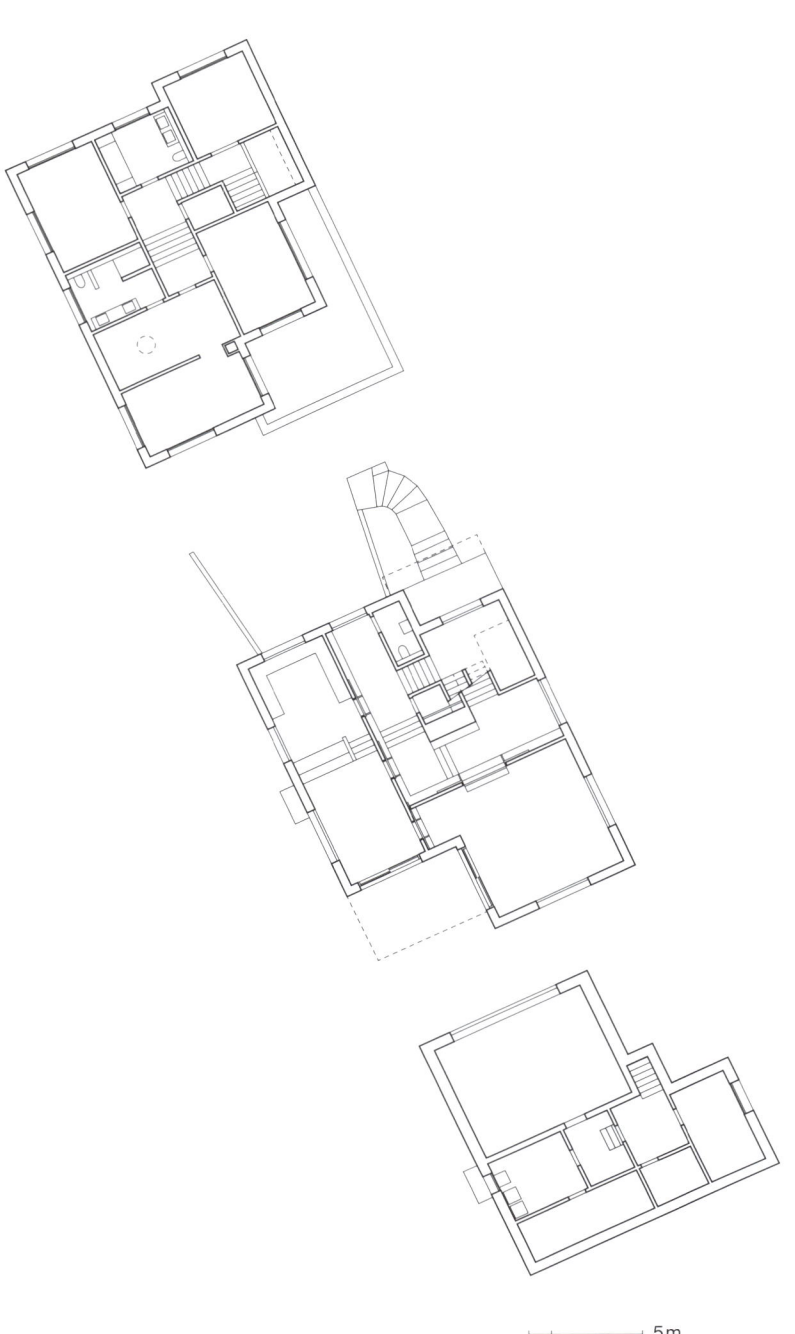

8 F

⊢——⊣ 5m

8 G

8H

8I